Adversity Leads to Achievement

Learning to Surmount Difficulties

Subesh Ramjattan, DHL, DLitt

ADVERSITY LEADS TO ACHIEVEMENT
Learning to Surmount Difficulties
Copyright © 2017 by Subesh Ramjattan

Library of Congress Control Number: 2017931891
Ramjattan, Subesh 1951—
Adversity Leads to Achievement
ISBN 978-1-935434-81-8
Subject Codes and Description: 1: BUS 046000—Business and Economics – Motivational; 2: FAM 030000: Family & Relationships: Marriage; 3: REL 012050: Religion: Christian Life – Love and Marriage.

This book was written in collaboration with Hollis L. Green and GlobalEdAdvance Press. All rights reserved, including the right to reproduce this book or any part thereof in any form, except for inclusion of brief quotations in a review, without the written permission of the author and GlobalEdAdvancePRESS.

Printed in Australia, Brazil, France, Germany, Italy, Poland, Spain, UK, and USA. Also printed on Espresso Book Machine© in various venues.

Book Cover Design by Global Graphics

The Press does not have ownership of the contents of a book; this is the author's work and the author owns the copyright. All theories, concepts, constructs, and perspectives are those of the author and not necessarily the Press. They are presented for open and free discussion of the issues involved. All comments and feedback should be directed to the Email: [comments4author@aol.com] and the comments will be forwarded to the author for response. Order from: www.gea-books.com/bookstore/ or subesh60@gmail.com or anywhere good books are sold.

Published by
GreenWine Family Books™
a division of
GlobalEdAdvancePRESS

www.gea-books.com

This book is dedicated to the
Alumni and Residents of

BRIDGE OF HOPE
Childcare

AND

OLIVE'S HOUSE
Eldercare

With a promise to provide
Quality of Life care

ADVERSITY LEADS TO ACHIEVEMENT

The struggle for a quality of life is to overcome daily difficulties and not be sidetracked from the planned course.

LEARNING TO SURMOUNT DIFFICULTIES

A BAKER'S DOZEN OF COMMON SENSE LESSONS

Why is a Baker's Dozen 13 instead of 12? The practice of baking 13 loaves for an intended dozen was insurance against a batch being lower that the statutory weight, which in some countries would cause the Baker to be fined. I have listed 13 Common sense Lessons learned from the past just to provide good measure.

1. Hard work is a necessary part of achievement.

2. The joint labor of two produces more achievement than one working alone.

3. Achievements can be made when one learns specifics about the cause of failure.

4. Never despair because of difficult work; it is a vital aspect of reaching established objectives.

5. Companionship and teamwork both support achievement, because "two are better than one."

6. Family and friend both have value because they are better than money in the bank and the benefits of true friendship are unlimited.

ADVERSITY LEADS TO ACHIEVEMENT

7. Learning the value of sharing, eating the same thing others eat, and wearing hand me down clothes are not misfortunes, but basic training for achievement.

8. Learning to earn, save, and spend money is a foundation for future achievement.

9. Learning the value of hard work and the worth of money is required to move foward in all aspects of life.

10. Patience is a virtue all must learn early to achieve.

11. Learning that life has a single focus provides a path to a lifetime of achievements.

12. Learning to value a gift by what it cost the giver is a great achievement.

13. Energy spent in a task increases the value in coinage the labor produces.

**Hardships often prepare
Ordinary people for
An extraordinary destiny...**

— C.S. Lewis

Contents

A BAKER'S DOZEN OF COMMON SENSE LESSONS		7
PUBLISHER'S PREFACE: Steps To Acquire A Purpose		11
AUTHOR'S INTRODUCTION: An Open Door of Opportunity		17
1.	Adolescent Lessons Span A Lifetime	23
2.	Parental Knowledge Brings Wisdom	31
3.	Business Setbacks Require Networking	37
4.	Selfish Behavior Demands Self-Discipline	45
5.	Spirituality Can Replace Religious Tradition	51
6.	Covenant Bond Surpasses A Contractual Union	59
7.	Enterprise Advances Business	69
8.	Connectedness Enhances Friendship	77
9.	Achievement Overcomes Negative Encounters	83
10.	Weak Leadership Breeds Discouragement	95
11.	Understanding Facilitates Wellness And Health	101
12.	Planning Ensures A Prosperous Lifestyle	107
ABOUT THE AUTHOR		115
AFTERWORD		117
RESOURCE BIBLIOGRAPHY		121
APPENDIX A: Adversity Response Profile (ARP)		123
APPENDIX B: Scoring: Adversity Quotient (AQ)		127
APPENDIX C: Adversity Quotes		131
APPENDIX D: Achievement Quotes		133
OTHER BOOKS BY THE AUTHOR		136

This book uses many passages of scripture, most of them from The EVERGREEN Devotional New Testament (EDNT). Debbie and I were among the sponsors of this translation and willingly share this devotional rendering of scripture. The frequent use of scripture was not only to support my words, but scriptures were added because God's Word says things better than this author can provide the language skills to communicate. Be patient and read each passage carefully; the message may not be readily seen. Ask the Holy Spirit for illumination of the Word. God bless you as you read, understand, and share the message of grace and love to all who will listen. We pray that each reader may be productive in turning adversity into achievement.

PUBLISHER'S PREFACE

Steps To Acquire A Purpose

Walking on the streets of Oxford, England with my oldest son, we saw graffiti scrawled on a college wall *"Life is not a paragraph."* Asking my son what it meant, his answer was clear "A paragraph is an idea fully developed and if you are alive, then you are not fully developed -- so life can't be a paragraph." Well, so much for those words of wisdom. Human development is progress over time and one must have a guiding purpose to stay on the determined course despite difficulties.

Purpose is considered the long-range reason and the general direction or focus for development. Purpose is always singular, because one cannot travel in two directions at the same time and a double-minded person is unstable. Sufficient to each day are the difficulties that all humans must face. The struggle for a quality of life is to overcome daily difficulties and not be sidetracked from the planned course.

As a young man, I had a motto on my desk *"Ideas are witty little things, but they don't work unless you do!"* Each morning I would think about this adage to get my creative juices flowing. Realizing that everyone had the same 24-hours in a day, I would consider how I could best accomplish the multiple tasks of the day by asking myself three questions: What can I do differently? What can I do better? What can I do new? Then when a notion, a thought, or an inspiration hit my brain wave, I would spin it around until it formalized into an "idea" worthy of my time. Perhaps this is why I became a writer: a paragraph is one idea fully developed. Here are my steps to acquire a purpose for the day and establish a long-range direction for life despite the normal difficulties:

Spin a thought into an idea.
Plant an idea and reap an action.
Repeat an action and gain a practice.
Produce a practice and harvest a lifestyle.
Achieve a lifestyle and acquire a purpose.

1. Spin a thought into an idea. The paragraphs of life consist of ideas. When ideas are fully developed, your words make sense to you and to others. Developed ideas give life meaning. Ideas do not work by themselves you must work with them to move your life forward. Ideas are curious little things that probe and pry at your intellect and must be planted and nourished to grow. An idea you have today may not work tomorrow. Ideas are short lived.

2. Plant an idea and reap an action. When an idea is firmly planted in the conscious mind, it will nourish deeds, even exploits that provide activities and undertakings that prepare the steps forward to assure advancement on the path toward progress. Often you may have to repeat the process to assure you are on a worthy path. Never neglect the power of replication, because repeating a process opens the mind to areas of concern and possible improvement.

3. Repeat an action and gain a practice. You have heard the saying, "Practice makes perfect." However, I am not sure this is true. It is true that repeating an action will establish a practice; although practice may make it better, it will not make things perfect. Almost every concept and construct conceived by the human element has flaws. No mere mortal, not even you, is always right, constantly wonderful, or immaculate. To err is human; therefore, you must always repeat the process to be certain you have found the best way forward. To gain a practice is to develop a process with procedures that minimizes human error and flawed thinking. The classic fields of knowledge were the practice of law, the practice of medicine, and practice of philosophy (that included religion).

The field of law has review by a higher court, medicine has the autopsy to determine malpractice or the cause of death and philosophy has the logic of Boolean algebra to determine the answer of "true or false." Personal behavior has the check and balance known as the human conscience. No process, procedure, or person produces a perfect lifestyle. Life is trial and error!

4. Produce a practice and harvest a lifestyle. Proverbs speaks to this issue, *"the breath of man is the candle of the Lord that searches the bottom of the heart"* (Proverbs 20:27 EDOT). It appears that lawyers send their mistakes to prison; medical doctors send their mistakes to the grave; and philosophers send their unanswered questions to the abyss of verbosity. Religion practitioners send their mistakes to judgment before the God of the Universe.

5. Achieve a lifestyle and acquire a purpose. Daily activities speak to lifestyle. It is a way of life, an individual routine, or a personal standard of living. It is this routine that determines your purpose in life: your reason for existing. It has to do with intentionality, which is the power of your mind to produce ideas and stand for values. It has to do with ideology, a combination of personal philosophy and theology that determine your social role(s) and ideas and values. It is at this combined level of intentionality and ideology that human beings work together to achieve positive social progress and purposeful control of their behavior. In my judgment, this is how you acquire a purpose in life in spite of the daily difficulties:

> *Spin a thought into an idea.*
> *Plant an idea and reap an action.*
> *Repeat an action and gain a practice.*
> *Produce a practice and harvest a lifestyle.*
> *Achieve a lifestyle and acquire a purpose.*

– Hollis L. Green, ThD, PhD, DLitt

LEARNING TO SURMOUNT DIFFICULTIES

One must correct the inferior before a superior can be constructed.

ADVERSITY LEADS TO ACHIEVEMENT

**In many ways
initial defeat is necessary
for long-term achievement.**

AUTHOR'S INTRODUCTION

An Open Door of Opportunity

Adversity often becomes an open door of opportunity for achievement. An old adage about life stated *"It is not what happens in life, but what one does with what happens that makes a difference in the kind of person one becomes."* A saying attributed to Napoleon about the hazardous struggle of battle is appropriate here, *"There is a time in every battle when both sides have lost --- victory belongs to the one who attacks first after this point of loss."* The lesson here was clear, when trouble comes one must take positive action to move past the difficulty. Loss can actually create the opportunity for gain. This common sense lesson from the past is most telling, *"Necessity is the mother of invention."* Difficulties can become stumbling stones to produce present failure or stepping stones to a positive future.

Faith-based principles can make a difference in a productive life. Starting with the Commandments from the Hebrew Torah and appearing in various forms in the sacred writings of most religions, common sense lessons are taught by moral scholars. One such lesson is recognized as a Golden Rule and moral leaders are stewards of both the instructions and the divine resources provided by Providence and preserved in sacred writings. The guidance of this Rule is so basic it is communicated in sacred writing in various forms:

- **Buddhism** –"Hurt not others in ways that you yourself would find hurtful." *(Udana-Vaarga 5, 1)*

- **Christianity** –"As you would that men should do unto you, do you also to them likewise." *(Luke 6:31)*

- **Hinduism** – "This is the sum of duty; do naught unto others what you would not have them do unto you." *(Mahabharata 5, 1517)*

- **Judaism** – "What is hateful to you, do not do to your fellowman. This is the entire Law; all the rest is commentary." *(Talmud, Shabbat 3id)*

- *Taoism* – "Regard your neighbor's gain as your gain, and your neighbor's loss as your own loss." *(Tai Shang Kan Yin P'ien)*

Lessons learned from parents and siblings growing up in a rural village, together with my education, work experience, and interpersonal communications in the real world, taught me to overcome difficulties: that adversity could ultimately produce achievement. It is such lessons that prepare young men and women to become parents and productive citizens. All the recorded accomplishments of history were the result of such learned lessons used to make achievements in spite of adversities and their accomplishments changed the world for the better. These common sense lessons became faith-based principles to guide my life and profession. They were used to create programs, construct buildings, change the hopes and dreams of disadvantaged children, restore dysfunctional families, provide age-specific education, and practical community service for those willing to learn. Such common sense lessons are transferrable and reproducible in other venues. If shared, these lessons could make a difference in the lives of families, communities, and society.

It has been said, *"God never wastes a hurt!"* We all have learned the hard way: we touched fire, spoke harshly to a friend, abused a relationship, developed hurtful habits, lived a less than perfect lifestyle, and as a result suffered many stumbling blocks. It is similar to this: a patient goes to a medical professional and says, *"When I raise my arm like this it hurts!"* and the response was *"Then don't raise your arm that way."* A story from early television tells of a young mother who asked an Interviewer *"May I say something to my young son at home?"* Given permission, she said *"Billy, whatever you are doing, stop it!"* It is natural for all of us to do things that displease others. The solution: stop it!

In sacred writings we find weak and failing individuals selected for a great work and this in spite of their shortcomings. God often chooses the weak to confound the wise or the young to overcome the strong. When one is divinely touched and called for a cause of action, the issue is not qualification; it is availability that counts. There is always enablement for those chosen for a moral cause. Even the faint of heart are used to accomplish great things for the good of mankind. Through the power of forgiveness and divine anointing, individuals are enabled to make positive achievements because God qualifies those He calls.

The sacred record is filled with individuals who failed at some aspect of their life or disappointed others by their behavior. Adam and Eve made a big blunder in the Garden, but God used them to start the human race. God trusted Noah to build the Ark that saved the seed family of humanity, but he got drunk. Abraham lied about his wife, but God used him to father a Nation. Jonah ran from God, but he was given a divine message for Nineveh. Moses was slow of speech, a stutterer, and had a bad temper, but God gave him the Law and used him to lead Israel out of bondage and servitude. David, the Shepherd Boy, felt unqualified, but God made him King; he then misused his position and power to take another man's life and wife. Surely, there were negative consequences to this behavior, but God still used him greatly.

Gideon was insecure and wanted a large army, but God limited him to a few good men (so God could provide the victory). Thomas was a doubter, but he saw and believed. Peter cursed, lied, and denied the Messiah, but God used him to strengthen others and lead the pristine group of believers. Saul of Tarsus persecuted believers and was struck down on the road to Damascus, but God used him as Apostle Paul to reach the Gentiles and trusted him to write one-fourth of the New Testament. Zacchaeus over-taxed the poor, but invited Jesus to his house and made restitution. Zacharias and Elizabeth stopped praying for a son, but God enabled them to become elderly parents of John the Baptist who prepared the way for the Messiah. God doesn't always call the qualified, but He always qualifies the called. God desires that believers live a life that is faithful to Him, not strive to be successful in the material world.

It is clear from my life experience that adversity can be overcome. Most of us have experienced what seemed to be impossible circumstances, but in reality they were great opportunities to use lessons learned and move forward. Also, I have learned from family and friends that failure is not the end, but a starting place for better things. Of course, real and lasting achievements do not come without hard work, but hardship and misfortune prepares the mind, body, and spirit of individuals and enables them to overcome future difficulties.

No mountain is too high and no valley too low, but that diligence and perseverance can bring accomplishments. God made both the mountains and the valleys, then man was made from the earth and told to "subdue, conquer, overpower, and overcome" the difficulties he would face. Consequently, mankind throughout the generations learned to surmount difficulties and grow a garden, build a home, raise a family, grow a business, develop a community, and establish Nations. The accumulated wisdom of the ages is preserved for those who wish to achieve their purpose in life.

– Subesh Ramjattan, DHL, DLitt

But we have this treasure in earthen vessels that the all-prevailing greatness of the power may be of God, and not from us. 8. We are repressed on every side, yet not hemmed in, we are bewildered, but never at a loss; 9. persecuted but not abandoned; knocked down, but never counted out;

(2 Corinthians 4:7-8 EDNT)

For I consider the sufferings we now endure not worthy to be compared with the glory about to be revealed in us.

(Romans 8:18 EDNT)

ADVERSITY LEADS TO ACHIEVEMENT

Each common sense lesson
prepares the young for a life
of teamwork and cooperation.

1

ADOLESCENT LESSONS SPAN A LIFETIME

During physical and psychological development usually known as adolescence, one learns the lessons that span a lifetime. Normally, as one moves toward physical and intellectual maturity, these common sense lessons become guiding principles for living. When adulthood is reached some abandon these principles or wait too late to map out their course for life. Others, as they face the difficulties of life, transfer some of the lessons learned into faith-based principles that continue to guide their lives throughout their entire lifespan. For others the hard lessons become stepping stones across troubled waters. Early life and career lessons should be remembered.

Evaluate how to deal with opportunities based on what you learned from your life experience and the hardships of the past. Life teaches many lessons but one stands out in my memory: the struggles of the past strengthened me for my future responsibilities. I learned that my behavior must change before my negative attitude about a situation or a person could change. It becomes clear to most adults that just changing your mind does not alter your predisposition to act in a given situation. Only by behaving differently could the present attitude toward difficult circumstances or unpredictable people be improved.

There is a story that comes out of Africa about how a young man becomes of age and his people see him as an adult. He is sent alone into the jungle to experience the difficulties of survival. As the lad faces the jungle darkness and the wild animals along his pathway to adulthood his strength and courage increases. When he slays a small animal, he considers his difficulty and gathers the strength to continue. As more and larger wild creatures are confronted, he continues to gain strength. Each time he overcomes a difficulty, his spirit grows and the victory adds to his strength and confidence. By the time his testing is completed, he returns to his village with the strength and courage that his struggle to survive brought to his mind and body. He was no longer a boy: he had overcome many hardships, survived conflicts with wild animals; he became an overcomer, and an achiever. He was now a hunter, a warrior, and accepted by his people as an adult and ready for future challenges. Such are the struggles of us all!

> **"Strength does not come from winning. Your struggles develop your strengths. When you go through hardships and decide not to surrender, that is strength."**
>
> **– Mahatma Gandhi**

The value of a charted course in life relates to both the terminal objective and the time one has to travel toward the end of life. A friend often says, "The end is worth the journey." Some lessons are used to establish a stable marriage, others are utilized to create a business; still others function to guide lifestyle behavior and the proper caring for children and the elderly. The reasonable thing to do would be to plan life early and permit the ultimate objective to guide your forward steps through the difficulties of life. Long range goals help one deal with short-term failures. If one fails to establish adequate life goals, personal and professional challenges could blot out the normal opportunities to advance the agenda for life.

My two older brothers, younger sisters and I, learned many lessons from our parents and other village families. Village life was an excellent learning experience. We grew watermelons in the Nariva Swamp. Holiday time for us was spent in the cocoa and coffee fields. We were also rice growers, so we milled rice in the family rice mill and milled rice for others for about a penny a pound. In order to earn extra money my eldest brother would borrow my father's vehicle to transport the local fishermen to the market. He got up at 1:00 am on Sundays to accomplish this task. These efforts gave us spending money for school and we learned common sense lessons from the ventures. The lessons learned from my family.

My parents were always able to manage with what little they had; sharing and giving from the heart were early lessons learned, and I saw what we had multiplied as they fed many others – we always had just what we needed. My father drove a garbage truck getting up at 4:00 each morning to do his job. Mother was a charitable person. I recall her giving raw flour and baking powder to villagers to make "roti" and she would bring them to the house for some salted butter to eat with the "roti." Mother operated a shop in the front of our house which was also the local post office. Honesty and integrity were the work ethics of my parents. They certainly lived up to John Wesley's words even in the midst of hardships, mother reminded us constantly of Wesley's words:

> **"Do all the good you can;**
> **By all the means you can,**
> **In all the ways you can;**
> **In all the places you can,**
> **At all the times you can;**
> **As long as ever you can."**

Memories of village life tugged at my heart and pulled me back to Trinidad and Tobago. My rural village suffered from isolation and we all learned early the need for cooperation and teamwork. Villagers realized that the joint labors of two produced more than the efforts of one solitary worker. From this we learned that companionship and teamwork were both supportive and profitable. These were common sense lessons learned from daily life in the village and this practical training enabled the realization that family and friends had dependable and lasting value. This brought a connectedness to our lives.

Small rural communities develop relationships that surmount difficulties and produce hospitability and warmth. This becomes a therapy and medication for many ills produced by poverty or isolation. Such interaction with a community spirit creates a good reward for a labor intensive culture. At times kindness becomes a reward itself, and the people of the village form lasting friendships. There is no end to the benefit of true friendship, especially those born out of difficult times. In fact, friends are better than money in the bank. One has access to their common interest without diminishing the value and resource of the friendship principal. Such relationships with friends and family provide assistance in emergencies, supply daily mutual support for families, and give additional strength for both the tasks at hand and the hard journey ahead. I will always be grateful to my family and the people in the village of Plum Mitan.

As a young man, my journey from a rural village to

developing studies and work experience was not an easy trip. Having won placement in Northeastern College, there were two main difficulties, first, after chores there was little space or time in a small house with a large family for study by kerosene lamps; this, together with transportation from the village limited to one 6 AM bus. Studying by lamp light and walking to the bus in the early darkness, I learned courage and perseverance and achieved five academic O-Levels, including one in the Principles of Business and Accounting. This became the foundation and motivation for me as a young man to venture into the larger world and dream of personally owning and operating my own business.

At age 18, with my parents blessings, a brown bag containing some clothes and food, and the generous gift of my father's last five dollars, I ventured out of the secure little village to the wiles of Port of Spain to seek employment and my destiny. With a tearful family parting and five dollars in my pocket, my father asked me to make a simple promise: *"Never steal from anyone."* Contained in the limited family resources represented by the five dollars and the moral promise never to take advantage of others by stealing was the essence of morality for my life and my practice of business. I did not have many skills but was willing and eager and common sense prevailed. With limited confidence I ventured into the unknown world in search of my purpose in life with the moral integrity to earn the resources to build my own business. The lesson that *"Honesty is the best policy in life and business"* has been a main stay for the moral principles used in business operations through the years.

Deep in the sacred Hebrew writings, one finds the story of an eagle teaching the young to fly. (Deuteronomy 32:11, 12) The story explained, *"As an eagle would* do this with their eaglet, so the Lord with His children." The people following Moses were accustomed to watching eagles as they soared above their camps. They also observed their nest building in the cliffs and the crags of the highest hillsides. They knew an eagle built a nest out of sticks and stones, sharp things, and then covered it with rabbit fur, down or fern to make a nice, soft bed for their hatchlings. The people were also aware of how the eaglets received their flying lessons. A brief review of that process could be instructive for those overcoming the difficulties of searching for the Right Path in life.

After the hatching of the eggs, the parents feed the eaglets regularly until they are small butterballs. Every time the eaglets hear the ruffle of a wing, they would close their eyes, open their mouths, and wait for food. The eaglets would prefer to stay in the soft nest the rest of their lives. It was soft, warm and comfortable with plenty of food and little or no conflict. However, the mother eagle was not satisfied with their failure to face the real world.

Moses described how the eagle *"stirs up"* her nest. After the nest was disturbed, she would flutter above her young. Normally, eaglets would just close their eyes, open their mouth and wait for food, but they were now uncomfortable. Sharp protrusions from the sticks and stones in the nest were now pricking their tender bodies, so when they heard the fluttering noise they opened their eyes. Then the eagle spread abroad her wings. Can you imagine the thoughts of the young eaglets? *"I never saw mother so big before."* Could it be that they had never looked. Some would venture up to the side of the nest to avoid the sharp things, others even to the edge of the rocks, but most were fearful of the drastic change coming to their life. Moses described how the mother eagle would take them, put them on her wings, and carry them high into the air.

The eaglet clutched to its mother's back on its first sky ride. It seemed easy, but all of a sudden the mother would jump from beneath the young bird and the eaglet would end up in free fall. Looking up at the majestic wings of their mother and feeling the wind catching the flapping weak wings on their sides, most would get the message, *"Hey, I had better do something about this!"* Then they would stick out their undeveloped wings in a feeble effort to hold back the wind. They could see the rocks and the trees coming up to meet them. They must have been frightened, but they tried. If the eaglet tried to fly, Job described how the mother would fold her wings and dart like an arrow beneath the fledgling eaglet, catch the young on her wings, and bear them up again. (Job 9:26; Exodus 19:4)

The eaglet probably thought, "I knew mother wouldn't let me down." Then mother would dump the eaglet into the air again, falling, and falling, and falling. The mother repeated this process until the wings were strengthened enough and the eaglet's courage was strong enough to flap and fly. Remember, the scripture recorded, *"As the eagle with the eaglets, so the Lord with His children."* This is a lesson we all must learn: we must remember what was taught at home and make an effort to achieve. Waiting on mother or God is not an answer. Those faced with a problem must act!

The other side of this coin is that if the eaglet did not try to fly, the mother would permit the young one to fall to the rocks below. Providence does use conflict and change to create an atmosphere conducive to growth and development, and this creative change can become a place of real achievement or it could become destructive. There is a choice: choose to use your roots and wings and venture into the unknown, or fail to use the door of opportunity and miss the chance to bloom where you are planted.

We gained courage and learned from failures; in fact, some time disappointments are the greatest lessons gained in life, or the failure to meet a desirable or intended goal. It became obvious as real life outside the security of home was encountered that life was not going to be easy. So we all tried to do our best, stayed busy in early work experience, learning everything we could each day. When we did our best, there was no time to worry about failure. When failures came, and they did, we all profited from the lessons learned and became more effective in our work and more confident about life. When trials, sickness, and disappointments came we turned to family and friends for encouragement. Their counsel usually taught us new lessons. Gradually from family and friends we learned wisdom and the courage to achieve in spite of difficulties.

Enduring hardship is a learning experience; maturity does not come easily; it is developed out of difficulties over time.

2

PARENTAL KNOWLEDGE BRINGS WISDOM

People are often unreasonable and self-centered.
Forgive them anyway.
If you are kind, people may accuse you of ulterior motives.
Be kind anyway.
If you are honest, people may cheat you.
Be honest anyway.
If you find happiness, people may be jealous.
Be happy anyway.
The Good you do today may be forgotten tomorrow.
Do good anyway.
Give the world the best you have and it may never be enough.
Give your best anyway.
For you see, in the end, it is between you and God.
It was never between you and them anyway.

–Mother Teresa

Observing a good example of parents and older members of an extended family are an encouragement for the young to act responsibly. Enduring hardship is a learning experience; maturity does not come easily; it is developed out of difficulties. The ancient sacred writings record that human beings are *"of a few days and full of trouble."* This fact of nature requires everyone to work hard at developing both patience with the human situation and staying power for life's journey. The ability to make progress is a worthy quality of a moral lifestyle. It is important that the positive virtues of moral examples from the extended family be obvious in the behavior and sacred memory of the next generation.

Developing long-ranged plans keeps one from becoming discouraged with short-term failure or temporary difficulties. When one is clear on a direction and destination, difficulties along the way may only increase the determination to press on to reach the objective. Projected life objectives become long-range goals to keep you from being frustrated by short ranged disappointments or personal failures.

The wisdom of good judgment is thwarted by the neglect of lessons learned from parents and the extended family. In the hurry-worry world of modern society, daily activities and hectic dealings seem to crowd out many constructive events and positive accomplishments. Not only were we neglectful in using the lessons learned from the past, these meaningful memories are often disregarded and discarded and hastily replaced by untested ideas from strangers or peers. Personal and systematic study of the moral and ethical process used by previous generations to solve problems must never be abandoned. A generalized boredom and social alienation are created by a life busy doing *"things"* without using foundational principles that leaves one seeking personal pleasure rather than striving to accomplish positive objectives. Perhaps we should follow the advice of ancient scripture:

> "Remember those that have the rule over you, who spoke the word of God to you; follow their faith, observe how they made their exit from this life."
>
> (Hebrews 13:7 EDNT)

It is truly a *"sad"* day when the younger generation does not listen to the good advice and follow mature guidance of the previous generation. Past experience and achievements are good indicators of positive change. Understanding a few symptoms of inattention could make one aware of this difficulty. Being a poor listener causes careless mistakes and a failure to follow through on important tasks. Such persons are easily distracted, forgetful of daily responsibilities, and have poor organizational skills. At times, Social Attention Deficit (SAD) causes restlessness with an inability to concentrate on important matters, this may cause one to act on sudden urges that weaken relationships and the ability to influence others in a positive direction. The excitement and lessons learned early from family often fade as one engages the daily challenges of life. When individuals encounter difficulties, it takes personal effort and courage to follow the primary course previously established by others. The objective is to move forward toward stated goals in spite of difficulties.

Human beings have a tendency to develop negative behavior that wipes out the possibility of future achievements. Many seem bent on self-destruction while others attempt to take down others to the lowest common denominator of life. At their lowest level, there are no steps upward, no ladder to the top, not a rope of hope and seemingly no redemption. Worse than any of the animal kingdom, the human race engages in behavior that ultimately destroys themselves and others, usually family and friends. They lie, cheat and steal, in the process of negative behavior that is hurtful to everyone around them. Lies often show deep psychological needs; such as, a lack of self-esteem or self-image. The fact that people cheat on their mates as well as their taxes, shows the scope and acceptance of negative behavior. Their eyes become accustomed to the darkness around them and willingly participate in the evil of the day. Some become involved in shady deals just for the thrill and the adrenalin rush. When individuals cling to bad habits; such as, gambling, gossiping, and bullying, they become sources of stress. This robs productivity and personal peace and greatly hinders moral advancement.

    The whole world cries out for role models, but few can be found. It was not a professional or a moral leader who brought to the attention of the world the need for good role models and good examples. It was William Shakespeare, an early English author, who called attention to those who had strong guidelines for others, but did not follow their own rules. He was concerned about the behavior of parents and moral leaders who had become "*good bad examples*" to the young. Although much of Shakespeare's literature is hard to appreciate, it appears that he clearly understood the human element that could intrude, interfere, and interrupt human communication and hinder moral advancement in society. Shakespeare was also aware that faith-based individuals often did not live up to their own standards.

    The gainsayers use any crack in the moral armor to dispute or contradict the moral cause of human welfare. All who choose to walk the path that leads to a better life or decides to lead in a moral cause must *"hold fast to that which is good"* and become a positive example to all concerned elements of society. When the mighty fall the other warriors flee. This is the tragic result of moral and ethical failure by past and present generations.

ADVERSITY LEADS TO ACHIEVEMENT

Difficulties can become stumbling stones to produce present failure or stepping stones to a positive future.

3

BUSINESS SETBACKS REQUIRE NETWORKING

Tragically, family and friends are not exempt from hardships and failures. Trouble is no respecter of persons; it strikes equally among the rich and poor. Sickness and death seem to be a repeated episode for each family. It is not what happens that counts; it is how one handles what happens that make the difference. The objective is not to take advantage of anyone, but rather to provide others an opportunity to join the cause, share in the mission, and develop support for a worthy project or an exciting adventure.

During this period I maintained my business in Trinidad and this allowed me to spend time with my parents, Rosie and Dipnarine, who lived in the peaceful country side. The sudden and unexpected death of my younger brother and business manager at the House of Marketing, Ltd. in Trinidad was a difficult time and happened when I was facing other real life challenges. God was tugging at my heart to reconcile my life with His will and to be concerned for the needs of others in my Homeland.

The loss of my brother was a heavy burden I could not carry alone. I had to reach out to friends to fill the void.

My new found faith and spiritual relationship with God enabled me to face these tragedies with an upbeat spirit and a purposeful determination to continue my progress toward making my business profitable. This required new and innovative network building to attract new business and increase the customer base. The loss of a close family member is always tragic and it is increased when the loss directly impacts your business and livelihood.

The setback caused by the death of my brother created a situation that required drastic action. It was now time for a fresh start in Trinidad. New management was hired for the House of Marketing, Ltd. and the business was expanded into other areas. I came to a decision to liquidate some assets and business in the United States so I could concentrate on my Homeland. These changes required many adjustments in my life, but I was thankful for divine intervention in my situation. I soon came to the realization that my Heavenly Father does not give His children a burden they cannot carry and with every difficulty provides a way forward within the bounds of His will.

Much energy and long hours of hard work were necessary to overcome the challenges at the House of Marketing, Ltd., but prayers were being answered. God was working and things were changing for the better. It was understood that prayer was not just getting the answer from God, but trusting and partnering with God with confidence that guidance for the journey was from above. The ancient sacred words of St. Paul informed my attitude:

> 1. As we work together with God, we appeal to you not to accept the grace of God and let it go to waste. 2. (God said, I have heard your prayers at a convenient time, and in the day of salvation I have brought you relief from a difficult

situation: observe, now is the time for coming together; now is the day of deliverance.

(2 Corinthians 6:1-2 (EDNT))

Networking with partners and building relationships to deliver goods and services became the order of the day. Identifying and describing the partners and assisting with various endeavors were a necessary part of the process. To identify the Government offices that cooperated and work with various projects; such as, Anapausis, Bridge of Hope, and Olive's House were not an easy task. It became necessary to identify and describe the organizations and groups that contribute to various aspects of the vision, and discover individual donors who would contribute to any of the enterprises or efforts advanced by the developing vision.

When some people think of a network, they assume it is socializing with men and women in fancy clothes, polite conversation and the exchanging of business cards, but I see social and business networking as a moral and ethical process of sharing a vision and a cause with people who are concerned about a common issue and have a sense of compassion for positive social change. In my estimation, true networking is an experience with people who are socially responsible and accountable for the support and progress of a worthy cause that benefits others. The process of working together for the needs of others is teamwork and partnering in meeting the needs of others. This is social and business networking and must be focused and guided by a sincere and redeeming motivation. The objective is not to take advantage of anyone, but rather to provide others an opportunity to join the cause, share in the mission, and develop support for a worthy project or an exciting adventure.

It takes a willing heart and cooperation to create positive social change. At times it means liquidating personal assets to cover promised business accounts. Removing debts and liabilities becomes a liberating experience and removes the load and concerns that had been using valuable time that should be focused directly on the High Calling placed on both heart and soul.

When the location and facilities of the House of Young Christians became untenable, it became necessary to purchase new land and build a new childcare facility known as the Bridge of Hope. This difficulty was transformed into a beautiful facility for the neglected and disadvantaged children of the region. The struggle to transition from an almost unusable building into a modern childcare facility was a most welcome change and it ushered in a new period of progress in serving the needy. This move also provided the land for the development and construction of Olive's House, a state of the art eldercare facility. The extra blessing was that many good people came along beside the staff and children and became stakeholders in a worthy project that has blossomed into a respected childcare and eldercare operation.

When the ancient people of the earth decided they would build a city with a tower whose *"top may reach even unto heaven"* (Geneses 11: 1-9), God saw the unity of the people and the sacred record notes *"now nothing will be restrained from them."* As long as they were in agreement and understood each other they were able to complete whatever project they started. When their motives became unclear, confusion developed. The lesson here is clear: unity is the route to achievement, and confusion is the path to failure. Individuals join a group or participate in a cause because they believe their personal goals will be met when group objectives are achieved.

If for a moment an individual thinks that personal goals will not be met, they will abandon the cause. Any loss of members or even silent resistance to positive change can cause failure in reaching constructive objectives. Those leading the process of change must be fully aware of both the attitude and action of all within the group. Otherwise, there will be unavoidable conflict instead of positive change.

The sacred record noted that when it came time to construct a tabernacle, the Hebrew people gave a willing offering so the work could be accomplished. *"We have more than enough materials on hand now to complete the job"* was the message of Moses. He declared *"no more donations were needed,"* (Exodus 36:4 TLB). Yet the willing heart gave more than enough, and Moses asked the people not to bring more gifts. We have not heard a similar statement in faith-based or community groups lately. In fact, if all moral and ethical members of the community supported worthy causes according to their means, the needs of children, young people, families, the elderly, and communities would be fully funded without appeals. Making a connection with others who may share the vision for a particular cause and perhaps share in supporting the cause with energy and effort is an exciting adventure. When people join together much can be accomplished.

Mountain climbers assist each other. If one slips and falls, the other prevents a disaster. Solomon, the wise Hebrew King wrote, "Two are better than one...if they fall the other will lift up his fellow... but woe to him that is alone when he falls for he has not another to help him up," (Ecclesiastes 4:9, 10). It took courage to climb that mountain, but it was character and integrity that shared the credit for the climb. Surely, those who demonstrate remarkable acts and show great courage or strength should be recognized, but the honor goes to all including members of the supporting network.

When Sir Edmund Hillary reached the top of Mount Everest, he was not alone. He and a Sherpa mountaineer, Tenzing Norgay, became the first climbers (1953) known to have reached the summit of the tallest peak in the world. When he returned to the base camp and met the press, the question was asked, *"Who was the first man to stand on top of the world?"* Hillary's answer was clear and concise, *"We were on the same rope. We got there together."* Why did Tenzing join Hillary on the climb to the summit of Everest? It was his job as a guide, but he also wanted to reach the top of the world. Hillary's and Tenzing's goals were the same and they worked together so both would arrive at the summit on the *"same rope."* Groups that work together must have the same goals.

A wealth of wisdom can be found in a dedicated group of individuals with a common purpose. Networking is one of the tools that can gather this wisdom and advance a common cause. Formalizing and maintaining friendly relationships with people is important to any cause. This is even more important when such friendships could bring advantages and opportunities to a cause or project.

When people work together as a unit and systematically discuss and plan for progress in a given area, great things happen. A cooperative network of people with a common cause can produce much more than a single effort. When a group of people truly enjoy working together to reach agreed upon goals, there is a synergy or extra effectiveness that occurs that is powerful. A group working together produces greater accomplishments because of the addition of individual capabilities. Networking combines extra energy and effort to assure greater achievements. A network is a group working to build and maintain friendly relationships that bring advantages to a cause or project. There is no room for selfish behavior in a family or business enterprise. When selfishness consumes one, there is great need for self-discipline and a change of lifestyle.

ADVERSITY LEADS TO ACHIEVEMENT

You may encounter many defeats, but you, must not be defeated. In fact, it may be necessary to encounter the defeats, so you can know who you are, what you can rise from, how you can still come out of it.

– Maya Angelou

4

SELFISH BEHAVIOR DEMANDS SELF-DISCIPLINE

There was a time when life was hectic and the pace was fast and the competition was fierce. It was starting to take a toll on my health and my family life. I felt lonely inside because something was missing. I did not have peace of mind. I did not concentrate on family, but was totally consumed with business and personal issues. My focus was on making money and more money. My life became confused and my candle was literally burning on both ends and I could hardly survive the night to reach daylight. Selfishness had consumed my life and there was great need for self-discipline and a change of lifestyle.

The concept of family as *"teamwork"* had become drastically altered in my life. For me *"team"* had become my side, my squad, my players, my business, etc., as if everything belonged to me alone. Team always represents a group of individuals working toward a common goal, and is always plural in nature. There is no place in teamwork for the personal pronouns such as, I, you, she, he or substitutes such as myself, her, me, or myself. Teamwork is not a *"me"* thing; it is a *"we"* effort and is always the cooperative work by a group.

This joint effort is collaboration and does not allow for personal credit. When two or more individuals work together to realize shared goals and the action is willing cooperation there are no personal accolades or hero awards, only mutual sharing of all benefits and responsibilities. God again began to water the seed planted as a child, during a major health crisis, and from providential circumstances through the years. On Parents Day we attended the sponsoring church of the school my daughter attended and I was surprised to receive benefit from the service. A few Sundays later I made a profession of faith and began to make more time in my schedule for the children and my new faith. I attended a New Believers study class that led to water baptism. The tender plant was growing. My life was slowly changing for the better. God had been working on me, now I was working on myself. Public worship, private devotionals, and study were moving my faith to a deeper commitment. It seems that God opens the door, but we must have the courage to walk through the love gate when it swings wide.

Attending a Christian Businessman's meeting, I was surprised at how happy the men were. I began to see a more pleasant side of life and my tender faith became strengthened. Providence had planted a seed of truth from sacred scripture, watered the seed with the kindness of family and friends, cultivated the tender plant with friendly and helpful medical staff, nourished the early growth during a period of recuperation, and strengthened a young believer through adversity and Bible study. Without clearly understanding what God had done, I was beginning an eventful journey from the House of Marketing, Ltd. to the Bridge of Hope and Olive's House. My concern for the needy children and eldercare was beginning to take shape and the sparks of the flame that later became the "*Anapausis vision*" was beginning to burn in my heart. I did not fully understand, but I knew clearly that something good was about to happen in my life.

Before a chaotic workday, I contemplated my future seated on the porch of my home near Miami. At the time, I owned seven businesses—three in Miami and four in Trinidad and Tobago, the southernmost island nation in the Caribbean Sea. I worked 15-hour days just to keep up with the demands. The stress made it difficult to sleep without medication. After one restless night, I began to think about how my life could be changed. I had seen Christian business people going through difficult times and maintain a pleasant disposition. This brought a discovery that the faith-based principles they used could be applied to my life and business. This was personally encouraging. My drive to make money became altered and I began to move in the direction of assisting the poor and my love for God started to grow.

Once touched by the hand of God, things had to change for the better. Moving from visiting bars to spiritual fellowship, my life seemed to take a new direction as I allowed God to become a reality in my life. Biblical studies became part of my daily routine and I started following faith-based principles from individuals who had used them in their personal journey. My predisposition to act began to change and I made new and better friends who became a constant source of encouragement. The old Friday evenings at the bars changed to a time of spiritual fellowship and study with the truest of friends. Self-discipline had taken hold and I was developing into a learner of moral and ethical ways to operate my business life and more particularly a better way to live my personal life.

The traditional behavior of men in my acquaintance had lost its hold on me. My eyes were opened to moral, ethical, and even spiritual matters. I began to think of what my life could be if my behavior continued to mature. The possibilities were exciting, even exhilarating. My new life was almost frightening; life was moving fast and faster. At first, I thought *"Stop the world I want to get off!"* Yet, the whole idea of spirituality was new to me, but I was beginning to see value in public worship, prayer, and reading sacred writings. This new spirituality was changing my life for the better. It was even replacing the bad parts of my culture and helping me establish new and positive goals for my children, my business, and myself. My eyes were opened; I could see myself clearly and could almost visibly witness how my changed life was moving me toward a Divine destiny. I began to ask, *"Lord, where does your cause need me most?"*

Growing stronger each passing day, my life story was beginning to look similar to a young African boy struggling to become a man. I understand from information out of Africa that for a young boy to become of age and function as a man, he had to overcome a series of difficulties. He was sent alone into the jungle to confront various wild animals. As increasingly larger challenges were conquered, each wild creature, in turn yielded up their spirit and strength and he grew increasingly stronger. After he overcame several wild animals, the accumulated strength and courage of each added to his own. Finally, he was able to confront anything in the jungle. Yes, he was still not fully grown, but he had gained courage and confidence from his struggles and was able to overcome the normal obstacles encountered in his life. He had become an overcomer because of his jungle experience. Life for most of us was similar. As various hardships, difficulties, and even opposition were faced boldly, we matured into a strong, self-reliant adult.

My newly found strength and confidence was giving me courage to act in a positive manner toward my children, my extended family, business partners, and fellow workers. I was beginning to overcome cultural limitations and replace old religious practices with personal spirituality. This newfound faith had become a conviction and I was agreeing with those who counseled and encouraged me. Real agreement was beginning to settle most of my doubts. True fellowship with friends became a reality. Spirituality may mean different things to different people, but for me it meant change *"Old things were passing away and most of my life was becoming renewed."* I was beginning to feel whole again. It was a great feeling.

ADVERSITY LEADS TO ACHIEVEMENT

Sometimes the smallest step in the right direction ends up being the biggest step of life. Tiptoe if you must, but take the step.

(unknown)

5

SPIRITUALITY CAN REPLACE RELIGIOUS TRADITION

Culture, language, food, music, and tradition often become mixed with religious practice. As such, religion becomes more form and style than true devotion to the one True God. As one matures and circulates in the world-at-large, they learn more about life and living. Existing beyond the limits of the extended family and personal household, views and behavior often change: sometimes for the worse and sometimes for the better. As individuals leave their parent's home, they begin to forsake some of the family traditions and this often includes some religious practices.

As individuals confront the harsh world of evil, betrayal, and "dog-eat-dog" competition, they begin to feel a need for the watch care of moral and ethical friends. This means they often seek out spiritual leaders that live and work in a different culture and faith-based group than their parents and extended family. This becomes an interpersonal conflict as one struggles between the past teachings of parents and the contemporary spiritual needs of the moment. Not wanting to go against tradition, people often turn to a broad concept called *"spirituality"* which provides some wiggle room within the particular practices. These perspectives bring a sense of connection to something larger than themselves.

Meanwhile, they continue to search for meaning in life which is a normal human experience. It may take months or even years for a transition from culture and tradition to faith-based spirituality. Often such individuals become more spiritual in nature but not necessarily religious in practice as they search for the right path to personal and spiritual well-being. Normally a spiritual awareness begins that *the end is worth the journey.*

To be spiritual is to search for meaning in life. Spirituality has to do with purity of motives, intentions and personal discipline. Personal growth normally brings a reformation to lifestyle where one seeks assistance from a Higher Power to accomplish their true purpose in life. Becoming spiritually minded is to seek to develop the Divine Nurturing Attributes with which one was born. God does not make junk and when an individual understands that their *"breath of life"* came from a Higher Source, they normally begin to acknowledge and appreciate divine intervention in their life.

Faith mixed with living develops meaning and purpose and one becomes open to a moral lifestyle and ethical behavior. Life is full of personal performance, group activities, and individual deeds in various relationships. Lifestyle has to do with the daily routine of everyday life and suggests a standard of living and a level of influence witnessed by the public. A moral lifestyle often is living a life in contrast to present friends. It clearly reveals to others the course of action that a person has charted for their life. When lifestyle is guided by a foundational faith, one normally walks on a new path and develops a new identity and self-image. A personal spirituality begins to develop. Developing a true spirituality may lead one to participate in an organized religion. At times, this process can become a difficult but exciting transition.

David in ancient sacred writings learned a great deal from the love of his father and his work with sheep. He developed a search for God and became known as a man after God's own heart, but he was still a man. He was a shepherd, but he went astray. Yes, he was strong and committed to defend the right. He even fought the Giant and won other battles. He reluctantly became a king, but he was still a human being. He was in the lineage of the Messiah, but he crossed the line and transgressed onto another man's territory. He had a man murdered so he could take his wife, and this brought great trouble into his life. As a troubled man, he prayed earnestly to a forgiving God as the verses below demonstrate:

> *"O God, my God! How I search for you! How I thirst for you in this parched and weary land where there is no water.*
> *How I long to find you!*
> *How I wish I could go into your sanctuary to see your strength and glory, for your love and kindness are better to me than life itself.*
> *How I praise you!*
> *I will bless you as long as I live, lifting up my hands to you in prayer. At last I shall be fully satisfied; I will praise you with great joy ,"*

(Psalms 63:1-5 TLB).

Asking God to bless in the scriptural sense is to seek a favorable intervention in your life, your family, and your present work. That is, when one seeks God's blessing they seek something beyond their human power to achieve or receive. Since it is God's blessing, one should leave the nature of the answer to divine wisdom; this is what Jabez did. When Jabez asked that his place in life be enlarged, he probably wanted to increase his area of influence, extend his field of operation, enlarge his lifestyle, increase his area of service, or even gain a larger gathering of resources.

Depending on the Old Testament translation in which one reads the Prayer of Jabez, they will find different words for his petition. What is clear is that Jabez wanted to change the concept of *"No gain without pain."* He wanted gain not pain. He wanted to change his self-image. Jabez was named because of his mother's birth pains, and now the past experiences of others were impacting his current self-image. His name actually meant *"sorrow."* Jabez requested divine intervention to change his life for the better by opening the way to a blessed future. It is a normal part of maturing as an adult to ask God to bless your future? The answer is just a prayer away!

Jabez did not want to dwell on the past or be limited by the thinking of others, but prayed with hope and anticipation for a better future. He wanted to live a more effective and expanded life. As some would say, Jabez wanted to live large for God. It was a positive prayer. Jabez had reason to be sad and depressed. Although his name meant *"sorrow,"* and the problems of the past were constantly on his mind. Yet he prayed a positive prayer that God heard and answered. The Prayer of Jabez is a good personal prayer to use daily.

> *9. Jabez was more well-known than his brothers, because his mother named him Jabez saying, I bare him with sorrow. 10. He was the one who prayed to the God of Israel,* **'Oh, that you would wonderfully bless me and help me in my work; please be with me in all that I do, and keep me from all harm and tragedy!'** *And God granted him his request.*
>
> (1 Chronicles 4:9-10 EDOT)

To neglect or delay an opportunity to grow and mature as an adult is to commit the sin of omission and limit the opportunity to serve the needs of others. About such oversight or lapse of responsibility, ancient scripture was clear: *"Therefore if a man has the power to do good things and fails it is sinful,"* (James 4:17 EDNT). Wrongdoing in any form is literally *"missing the mark"* and becomes an offense against both God and man. This comes from understanding the early terms used in archery. When the arrow failed to strike close to the center or missed the target altogether, the arrow *"missed the mark"* and this became known as *"sin."* There is no excuse for the sins of neglect. Such failure may be avoided by personal prayer and dedication: a simple move toward personal spirituality.

The life you live day by day can make a difference in how you influence those around you. The constant and consistent prayer should be, *"Lord, help me give you first place in my life every day."* We are warned that *"sufficient to each day is the evil"* so it is vital that the troubles and sorrows of the past not be carried over to the daylight hours. Each believer must prepare adequately before sunset for the opportunities and personal responsibilities at the sunrise. To awake without adequate thought and preparation for the day is to limit accomplishments. When Providence permits us to see another day, it is because there is additional accountability for the opportunities afforded. One should always remember, *"Opportunity equals obligation."* To do the right things and reverence God is not an option. This is the pathway from trouble and sorrow to blessings and a positive lifestyle.

The light of a new day provides each person with both the authority to act and the responsibility to behave in a moral manner. Using all favorable conditions to present spiritual benefits to others and advance positive social and spiritual change is the action of a mature person. The story of the Good Samaritan tells of a Priest and a Levite, *"each by chance,"* had an opportunity to serve a man in need, but did not see either the opportunity or the obligation. Another man of low estate came by and ministered to the man who had been robbed and wounded. He was not a religious worker; he was a traveling salesman (a businessman). Sacred writings called this man *"good"* even though he was considered second-class by the social and racial standards of his day. God uses a willing soul to serve the needs of others. It is not position or station; it is simply availability that counts with God. To be blessed, take advantage of each and every opportunity to assist others.

Since Genesis (1:11,12) taught us that the *"seed is in the fruit,"* and each plant, animal, or human being reproduced its own kind, we should also understand that if a Mango tree produces mangoes, or monkeys reproduce monkeys, we should be aware that God said, *"Be fruitful and replenish the earth."* God places each of us in the *"soil"* where we can best grow, develop, and reproduce. In this light, a spiritual person should reproduce spirituality in others. How is your reproduction? It is vital for those who would serve the needs of others to look closely around where they live and work. God expects you to grow and bloom where you were planted. Do not go *"some place"* looking for an opportunity to serve or share; look closely around you for opportunities to do good things. What about family, friends, neighbors, workmates, and the needs of your own community?

A mature person should never forget that opportunity presents them with responsibility. Where there is a need, you must fill it. Where there is hate, you must show love. Where there is hunger, you must supply food. If one is homeless you must find them a place to sleep. If one is lost you must show them the way to the right path in life. To grow and bloom yourself, you must always act when and where there is a need.

In fact, the best definition for sharing good news is *"meeting someone at their point of need."* The meeting of a needy person requires action; usually this action is urgently needed. A spiritual love and a sense of caring must be manifested without delay, and the efforts must meet the need. Seek first the spiritual Kingdom; then you will be ready to meet the needs of others.

> *17. For yourselves, beloved, be warned in time; do not be carried away by their impulsive errors, and lose the firm foothold you have won; 18. But grow up in grace, and in the knowledge of our Lord and Savior Jesus Christ.*
> *To Him be glory; now and for all eternity.*
> *Amen.*
>
> (2 Peter 3:17-18 EDNT)

ADVERSITY LEADS TO ACHIEVEMENT

As individuals leave their parent's home, they begin to forsake some of the family traditions and this often includes some religious practices.

6

COVENANT BOND SURPASSES A CONTRACTUAL UNION

Two types of marriages exist today: first, those who hurriedly wed, usually with the wrong motives and without planning for a long life together. Those who do advance planning, receive pre-marital counseling, and make personal covenants with each other intend to live together in a lifelong fruitful relationship. Normally, one is civil and the other religious; however, many have religious weddings without the bonding of two souls necessary for a *"till death do us part"* commitment. In fact some civil ceremonies use the phrase *"as long as you both shall love"* rather than *"as long as you both shall live."* As individuals mature and grow together by raising a family, they either break the contractual arrangement or mature the relationship into a true covenant bond. The weakness of the contractual union (civil) is that it takes two to make a contract, but one can break the contract without the consent of the other.

When God looked at a lone man in a beautiful Garden, the divine understanding was, *"It is not good for man to be alone."* This brought about the need for a suitable *"helpmate."* It is clear from this and all of history that everyone needs the friendship and assistance of others to accomplish anything worth human effort. God places individuals together not only to help each other but to work together for the good of others. Unless one lives a life larger than their self-interest, they will never be comfortable working together with others to meet the greater needs of mankind. Positive social change will come only through the cooperative efforts of many. This requires a networking of friends and family.

Although I did not always feel this way, deep in my heart there was hope that someday I would meet someone who had a similar childhood and comparable youthful struggles as my upbringing, and we could together have a meaningful life. With the loss of a contractual union and my growing concern for my children, the hope for a better future was developing. Knowing that struggles produced unpleasant lessons and practical principles, I began to hope for a better and broader future and began thinking of returning to Trinidad, my Homeland. Today I realize that returning to my Homeland was part of a divine masterplan for my life. Now those lessons are working for me and my soul mate in socially sensitive, non-profit endeavors and in profitable business ventures. God's plans are wonderful.

With my personal problems on the back burner, I returned to Trinidad from the United States to use my wealth, wisdom, spiritual strength and faith-based orientation to benefit my Homeland. Problems could wait or be solved in the process of constructive change. When a true soul mate came into my life and covenanted with me in a lifelong venture to serve God and assist our Homeland, good things began to happen. I celebrated my birthday on January 25, 1994 and the next day Debra Frost entered my life. On Christmas Day, 1994 I received a precious gift and a life partner with covenant marriage. Debbie became a true partner and companion in my spiritual journey to assist distressed children, broken marriages, dysfunctional families, and needy communities of our Homeland.

God was still equipping and urging me forward toward a new and better lifestyle and a more unselfish view of business. Teamwork was the founding principle that guided the planning to care for needy children and the elderly as a foundational step to improving family life. The process of looking to the future of Trinidad and Tobago provided unlimited opportunities for service. In the process of taking advantage of opportunities, various needs were uncovered and plans developed to solve individual, family, community, and societal problems. Each known opportunity became an open door and the passage through which Debbie and I walked together to serve others. Good things do come to those who trust, hope, and wait till God opens the door of opportunity. Knowing that God answers prayer; sometimes He says *"Yes"* at other times He says *"No"* and at still other times God says *"Wait!"*

God brought us together not only to help each other, but to work in a covenant bond for the good of others. A God-fearing spouse means a faith-partner and that the two of us would have a good reward for our faith-based labor. We could now live a life larger than ourselves and work together in areas of the greatest need. Debbie was truly a gift from God.

Finally, I had a prayer and faith partner. When two agree before the Lord on a direction, powerful things can happen. Partners become accountable to each other and true companions on the journey toward spiritual fulfillment. We have come to realize that marriage is a faith-based contractual relationship; it is a covenant bond where each one must give up something to gain incredible blessings. Could this kind of spiritual partnership be a fulfillment of a statement in the journal of a young missionary killed by the Auca Indians in Ecuador* many years ago? A page from his journal was found floating in the river: *"A man is no fool who gives up what he cannot keep to gain what he cannot lose.*

*Operation Auca was an attempt by five Evangelical missionaries to bring Christianity to the Huaorani people of the rain forest of Ecuador.

Seeing a spouse as a gift from God is necessary to develop a spiritual partnership. *"Can two walk together except they agree?"* True partnership with one's life-mate is a prerequisite to spiritual involvement with faith-based programs and projects that produce positive social change. It is this *"true and faithful partnership"* that supplies the grace, encouragement, and support required to be involved in faith-based projects that have positive influence on the community and the Nation at large. True partnership makes good things happen!

Growing up in different villages of Trinidad but sharing similar lessons and principles for life, surely our meeting and becoming partners were designed by God. Based on childhood and youthful struggles, we were both committed to changing the future of children, young people, families, and the elderly within our sphere of influence. Somehow a plan came together that became evident to both of us. It was a plan as simple as A. B. C. and 1. 2. 3. The business plan that would fund the charity projects and the social programs required hard work and sacrifice of time and energy. To fulfill the noble mission and our joint vision for our Homeland we needed divine assistance as well as the support and partnership of individuals and stakeholders in the corporations of Trinidad and Tobago. What was this simple plan?

1. *Affection for children, families and the elderly;*
2. *Business established on faith-based principles;*
3. *Contacts to build a resource network.*

It is important to have a working partnership. Could it be the lessons and the practical business practices we learned in the villages of Trinidad or the personal struggles and the early work experience that prepared me, and Debbie, to meet the criteria for companionship and a covenant marriage? Could it be that we grew and developed in the same soil and learned compatible lessons and common business practices to become working partners in moral adventures to improve the plight of children, families, the elderly, and communities in our Homeland? We have come to believe the teamwork and relationship that has developed was more that accidental; it was part of a grand design to prepare two individuals who could produce a workable vision for positive benefits and constructive social change. Achievement is always a partnership.

All growth requires adjustment and change and the marriage relationship is no different. Marriage is a close and intimate bond that produces both challenges and opportunities. The familiarity that marriage brings to a relationship may at times produce friction, but that is when faith-based thinking works to produce a better and more productive relationship. Much as an oyster with a grain of sand in their shell would cover the irritation with layers of nacre, also known as mother-of-pearl, until the iridescent gem is formed. Likewise, the marriage relationship is normally able to overcome the irritation of human weakness with special layers of maturity and assistance from a Higher Power. Each marriage has its own string of pearls that demonstrates perseverance and patience. With most marriages, adjustments and challenges are faced during the early years of marriage.

As our marriage relationship matured, we came to understand that God often turns difficulties into lessons learned. These lessons advance the relationship journey along the path of faith. Adversity often leads to advancement and loss becomes gain. A lesson learned that can be applied to most achievement is often repeated in many areas of life: *"No gain without pain."*

Providentially, Debbie and I were introduced to Family Life materials and principles taught by Campus Crusade. The first principle was defeating selfishness; which caused us to examine ourselves and once we worked through this one, it became a wellspring for the others. These materials encouraged us to get involved in Family Life, a ministry of Campus Crusade for Christ. Family Life offers a series of life building products and programs. Home Builders are interactive sessions where couples meet and together discuss the principles of marriage. Valuable lessons are learned so couples do not have to endure relationship battles without ammunition. A marriage mate is not an enemy but a gift from God. Since God does not make junk, couples must learn to value each other. This was a good lesson Debbie and I learned that made a difference in our lives and work.

The love was mutual and as the relationship grew the vision and mission were expanded. We started pursuing the things of God together and began to see more clearly our purpose and calling in life. Even the earning of money had a lofty purpose and was somehow connected to the vision. We began to seek divine strategies to clear debts and restructure the business enterprises in Trinidad. True love changes the attitude, the predisposition to act, and new and better lifestyle is forth coming from a committed relationship. Working together with God is a good place to be in life and work. We learned from Scripture in Amos 3:3 that there must be agreement for two to walk together in harmony. This kind of spiritual unity and togetherness enabled us to walk in spiritual agreement. This teamwork made the journey worthwhile and more productive.

> *Love has no room for fear; and indeed, love drives out fear and when it is flawless, love drives out the punishment of fear;*
>
> (I John 4:18 (EDNT)

Marriage partners must agree to disagree agreeably. This requires either a written or spoken agreement that is in reality a covenant that reduces the tension, narrows the differences, and expands the possibilities of taking advantage of opportunities. To create a true partnership, such understanding and agreements are necessary. Love alone is not sufficient to hold a relationship together; the human element always puts a *"fly in the ointment."* Such a mutual agreement requires both partners to constantly repair and regularly mend any broken fences, and at times nurture the healing of a broken heart. When this occurs, marriage becomes a productive union with the blessings of Providence, and the cause of morality is advanced. Marriage may not be perfect, but it is much better than the aloneness that comes with the alternative.

Subesh and Debbie Ramjattan

Notwithstanding all its dysfunction and embarrassments, the marriage relationship is a blessing. In most cases, a soul mate is better than being alone, because celibacy is normally considered to be abnormal and requires a consecration that most are unwilling or unable to make, especially in this sexually charged, self-indulgent society. At creation it was clearly stated, *"It is not good for man to be alone."* Sacred writings made it clear that it was better to marry than to attempt to contain the passions of the flesh. Marriage can be a blessing that brings morality and stability to individuals, the family, and the community.

A stable marriage also becomes a blessing to faith-based groups because it opens many doors of opportunity to both men and women to be involved in building a moral society. Marriage also enables a meaningful experience with faith and a team approach to growing good families, good communities, and a positive agenda compatible with positive social change.

Relationships are based on an agreed covenant that requires a willing compromise. Originally, *com - promise* was a mutual promise coming from the word "*com*"- together with, and "*to promise.*" The parties agreed to adjust and settle a difference by mutual consent, with concession on both sides and to surrender one's own self-interest to gain a benefit. In a spiritual sense this is the faith-based aspect of the ministry of reconciliation. This requires both parties to mutually agree and promise together that each will give up something to achieve a better life together. God brought us together, not only for mutual benefit, but also to work together for the good of others in our Homeland.

- "Your spouse is a gift from God."
- "Two are better than one for they have a good reward for their labor."
- "God put us together not only to help each other, but to work together for the good of others."
- "A God-fearing wife means a faith-partner."
- "Live a life larger than yourself and work together with God in the areas of the greatest need."
- "Strength does not come from winning. Your struggles develop your strengths. When you go through hardships and decide not to surrender... that is strength."

ADVERSITY LEADS TO ACHIEVEMENT

One mark of successful people is they are action-oriented. A mark of average people is they are talk-oriented.

–Brian Tracey

7

ENTERPRISE ADVANCES BUSINESS

Just as a child cannot nurture itself, a business cannot function by itself. Since it takes a family and a community to bring up a child; it takes an extended family, close friends, customers, and a network of stakeholders to create, support and operate a business enterprise. Just as a child needs parents, an extended family, school teachers, health and medical people, faith-based groups, and a friendly government to grow and become a productive citizen, a business needs a similar network of corporative stakeholders. Normally, after several years of business operation, the owner begins to delegate responsibilities to others. When this happens, the proprietor usually steps back to take it easy believing that all is well. Then the unexpected happens: an economic downturn, the loss of customers, the leaving of longstanding employees, or some untoward scheme happens to siphon off the customer base.

When such things occur, it is time for drastic action. This usually means some form of innovative enterprise: a project that is important and difficult and requires boldness and energy. In terms of a business the word *"enterprise"* has value for both the business and the customer. The concept of *"enterprise"* is best understood by using the archaic spelling *"enterprize"* and dividing it into two words (enter-prize). How does a business get new customers to *"enter"* the facility and what benefit or *"prize"* will the customer receive. When a downturn comes to a business or the brand is damaged in some way, it is time for a bold push toward previously unused solutions; things that were not necessary before but now are required to maintain operation.

How could such things happen; for instance, a faithful and trusted leader, trained to assume a key-man role in the business, decides to go on his own and draw off part of the customer base? Such a difficulty causes one to revert to the basic plan that started the business and grasp for ways and means to survive. When one door is closed; another one is opened. Unexpected setbacks can become an open door to a combination of favorable or advantageous circumstances that lead to expansion and greater progress.

The loss of a long standing employee who became a competitor created a difficult time for my business. All who would do honest business must keep their promises because *"your word is your bond."* Dependability is the proper word and one that is expected of a loyal employee. It is a similar concept as the one used to describe a reliable and trustworthy man in sacred writings *"And I will fasten him as a nail in a sure place,"* (Isaiah 22:23). When a business has no reason to doubt the faithfulness of a long time employee, and there is a sudden disruption, both the cash flow and the equilibrium of the business are disturbed. When the *"nail in a sure place"* becomes <u>*a loose screw*</u> in the floor of company leadership, the sudden loss can work havoc in the business. When such an event happens, the proprietor may find the business keys on the ground and the door locked. Aggressive enterprise is required to move forward.

A business is a venture or risk on the part of all stakeholders, but for the public it must be dependable as a fixed asset with an air of permanency. The essential elements of business require the venture to be relevant and relational. A business is an organization, and therefore, the principles that work in an organized faith-based group also work in a business. In fact, shepherd management and servant leadership used in a non-profit enterprise and faith-based group also work in a commercial establishment.

When leaders with fixed dependability suddenly change, drastic measures are required for a business to remain relevant to the community, employees, and customer base. The company must maintain an appropriate structure, with useable and applicable products, and a longstanding customer base. If the brand is soiled or significantly damaged, the business must immediately become a new enterprise. A business is not effective just because it exists, but because among others it stands out as a dependable *"brand"* with a category of products desired by the customer base. When that *"brand"* denotes stability, the customer base is retained, but when the *"brand"* is damaged the customer base and cash flow is at risk. Such a business must be ready to engage in daring and challenging action.

My business had expanded rapidly until the economy of most of the world went through a recession including Trinidad and Tobago. Many owners of local businesses sold their properties and migrated to the United States or Canada. During this economic downturn, I moved temporarily to the United States so my children could enroll in school. This was when my life began to change for the better. My daughter attending a faith-based Christian school was the beginning of this change in attitude and lifestyle. The move was primarily for my children, but it had divine consequences. God was arranging my life so I could come to know Him more intimately and be prepared for the final stage of work and service to the needy in the land of my birth.

It was time to get back to business and family basics. Honest business practices started with my father's admonition, *"Never steal from anyone."* Mother's rule *"16 ounces is 16 ounces"* were the openness and integrity of my basic business and lifestyle model. I tried to teach those who worked with me to *"Under promise and over deliver."* Also, I wanted those who worked with me to understand that honest work deserved honest pay. Hopefully, the workers would catch the spirit of giving and sharing and understand that they could not give what they did not possess. Hard work then became a means not only to support myself and my family, but it provided both the ways and means to assist others and their families.

If my vision to assist needy children, the elderly, and work for the common good of families were to be accomplished, there had to be significant resources. Being a businessman, my first thought was to use my skills to generate funds to support worthy projects. Then I realized that I needed partners to come along side and assist with the task of funding these special efforts. I needed an enterprising network to move my business enterprises in a new and profitable direction.

When something happens to alter the cash flow, where goods and services are exchanged, a readiness to engage in daring or difficult action is required. The standard key to progress is a broad and comprehensive overview of the business plan and basic concept of family and lifestyle. This outlines what the business does and how it will be operated, covering everything from funding to dealing with markets and competitors. What market needs will it satisfy? Whom will the business employ and serve? When the marketing and leadership keys are used in a non-profit or faith-based project, they are multiplied by divine blessings. There is personal benefit and satisfaction in assisting others in need. Paying past blessings forward is a worthy goal. Somehow it is true what the old Preacher said, *"Cast your bread on the waters and it will return with butter and jam."* Helping others is a sure route to business progress and personal satisfaction for workers and all stakeholders involved in the venture. The dozen keys below unlock the secrets of a prosperous and progressive business.

1. Detail the ideas that would attract potential partners.
2. Provide the framework for what the business is about.
3. Identify the target market and its needs.
4. Isolate a possible competitive edge.
5. Name the service/product to be produced or marketed.
6. Describe the day-to-day operation.
7. Project expected income and cash flow.
8. Name the leadership and management team.
9. Plan for a productive work environment.
10. Maintain a stable customer base.
11. Constantly seek ways and means for expansion.
12. Plan for profits to be shared with workers and the needy.

The House of Marketing Ltd. became a major supplier of building materials operating with three branches. The company operation has been effective for over four decades and local professionals have increased the business and import capacity to better serve the customer base. The House of Marketing, Ltd. gained international recognition and reputation which allowed foreign suppliers to provide products to market in the Caribbean.

It is similar with individuals who need strong personal and social connectedness to enhance their relationships with others. The associations and partnerships create a sense of wholeness and linked relationships that endure. Social connection bonds people together and normally enables individuals to see how things work. Faith in a company creates respect and almost every event has a reason. This opens the door to true friendship and enduring alliances.

ADVERSITY

"The most beautiful people we have known
are those who have known defeat,
known suffering, known struggle, known loss,
and have found their way out of the depths. These
persons have an appreciation, sensitivity,
and an understanding of life that
fills them with compassion, gentleness,
and a deep loving concern.
Beautiful people do not just happen."

– Elisabeth Kubler-Ross

ACHIEVEMENT

"My grandfather once told me that there were two
kinds of people: those who do the work and those
who take the credit. He told me to try to be in the
first group; there was much less competition."

– Indira Gandhi

ADVERSITY LEADS TO ACHIEVEMENT

A society grows great when old men plant trees whose shade they know they shall never sit in.

–Greek Proverb

8

CONNECTEDNESS ENHANCES FRIENDSHIP

Connectedness has great value. Leadership, workers, and all stakeholders in a business have a link to the past and a bridge to the future through a connectedness. It is important to remember that the business that provides both "roots" and "wings" also provides the means to make positive social change in all connected constituencies. Many things are important in life, but the talents and services provided by a business are the glue that creates the connectedness which holds the operation together. Each person involved in the operation must utilize their time, skills and talents to make the business profitable. This is a continuing responsibility of everyone involved from the janitor, to the salesforce, to the management, and must not be neglected. Just as a tree has as much growth in the roots as it does in the foliage and fruit bearing area, a business must be managed to enable the roots to produce reasonable profit.

Individuals with strong links to others, normally see purpose and value in maintaining each relationship. Whether it is a friendship connection or a business link, feeling connected benefits the attachment with acquaintances. An individual with strong social connectedness enhances their friendship relations at an individual level and increases the quality and strength of the linkage. This is true in the business environment, in families, in faith-based groups, and in personal relationships.

Just as an extended family is to a child, a social and enterprising network brings connected benefits to business. Being linked to friends and colleagues is a great asset to well-being and linkage with a customer base. Stakeholders are an essential part of any business. Self-centeredness and self-interest are two blights on any personal or business connection. True friendship is actually directing interest and value toward another, but when selfishness turns a person to selfish acts, a relationship or a business enterprise is in trouble. Whether the connection is based on social chemistry customer base or friends, selfishness can destroy a relationship.

Honest caring for others brings a self-sacrifice that may require the giving up of personal wants and even needs for the benefit of others. Unless selfishness is defeated, a fractured relationship is doomed. Those who would defeat selfishness must persevere and be steadfast of purpose in all aspects of life. A proper relationship prompts one to abandon personal wants for the benefit of others: a spouse, a friend, a family member, or a coworker. There is no place for selfishness in a relationship or any joint endeavor. Partners should become good friends, worthy companions, and honest colleagues. True friendship should operate much as a family: for the good of the whole. This creates positive examples for all concerned.

Some individuals because of weak conditions develop a poor self-concept, and this produces a weak self-image. Those with a poor self-image normally project that faulty image to other human beings. The big question is: have those who do not believe in a personal God projected this construct to others and to the world at large? If so, has this projection created a secular environment without moral and ethical values?

If this were true in a circle of friends, what can be done about this tragic state of affairs? The best way is to limit your involvement and find another group with which to associate.

In the days of artificial sugar, substitute butter, tofu, and other substitutes for the real things, everyone needs to associate with people who are true, realistic, authentic, accurate, believable, and true to their word. Whether we win the game or are triumphant in a project, it is faithfulness that overcomes life's major difficulties. It is reliability and trustworthiness that produces positive social and reasonable profits. It is authenticity and truthfulness that produce an atmosphere that enables growth and material gain. The Prophet Isaiah wrote about peace and trust,

> *"You will keep him in flawless peace,*
> *whose mind waits on you:*
> *because he trusts in you,"*

(Isaiah 26:3 EDOT).

Look beyond the challenges of disrupted business, or broken relationships to the potential for a better life. When people are out of order and their lives are not working, someone must step in to put the pieces together again. Often broken lives are similar to Humpty Dumpty where all the Kings men could not put things together again. Notwithstanding, we are not building an earthly kingdom; we must work together with a Higher Power to mend broken hearts, put the pieces of a fragmented life together again, and make the situation better than before whether it be a downturn in business or a failed relationship. We must recognize fixing things is often beyond human ability and we must be open to divine intervention. The power and work of the divine is able to create an environment and way of life more responsive to restoring a relationship or reconciling a conflict. Those who believe in God's love and concern for His people must be aware of divine concern for a faith-based group, a family environment, or a business enterprise. God does not limit blessings, He works anywhere flawed human beings function.

It is my firm conviction that when individuals and families show proper concern for one another, the path to a life of quality is opened, but they must choose to walk on that pathway. When individuals neglect themselves, their children (or other people's children), and their parents or the elderly parents of others, they are on a slippery slope on which the end is misery and disappointment. My personal conviction is that a quality of life bridge can be constructed to assist each child, every family, and all who will willingly follow divine guidance. This bridge over the troubled waters of life can improve both personal and professional relationships. This greatly enhances the quality of life for those involved.

As the quality of life increases, individuals become more positive in their relationships. This paves the way for real advancement and progress in many aspects of life. The bridge from negative thinking to a positive outlook is a major advance toward real achievement. Progress in any endeavor enables one to overcome negative encounters that sidetrack their advance. When one feels linked to others, they gain strength for the journey. Since two are better than one; then three are better than two, and the count goes on exponentially. Perhaps the saying, *"The more the merrier"* suggests that the more connected one feels toward others increases a positive outlook on life and relationships.

As the quality of life increases, individuals become more positive about their relationships. This paves the way for real advancement and progress in many aspects of life.

ADVERSITY LEADS TO ACHIEVEMENT

The place God calls you to be is the place where your deep gladness and the world's deep hunger meet.

– Frederick Buechner

9

ACHIEVEMENT OVERCOMES NEGATIVE ENCOUNTERS

Negative encounters become struggles that must be overcome in the battles of life. Achievements are accomplishments in spite of these battles. Some would call these *"victories"* or positive endeavors. Victories are always incremental. Progress is made in phases or steps and small in comparison to the size of the project or the length of the journey. There are small positive or negative changes in individual lifestyles that are obvious. When sacred scripture becomes a mirror in which individuals see themselves the way God sees them, often their behavior changes. There is always room for improvement and the small steps should come with daily effort to measure behavior in terms of moral and ethical standards.

Physical and moral development is always in phases. The life span from birth to death illustrates the stages of human development. First, there is intellectual awareness, then physical growth and development, then spiritual awareness and favor with Higher Powers. After spiritual awareness comes social adjustment and improved human relationships. These stages represent mental improvement and physical development, then behavior that is acceptable to God and finally social development and acceptable behavior to others. Developing the mind and body and a personal relationship with God must come before social development. Otherwise, one permits others to bring negative influence to embellish their moral and ethical lifestyle. However, one's relationship with God is uniquely personal and does not require a human go-between. Failure in this logical development causes flawed function in business and life.

Debbie and I planned three crucial phases for projects in our Homeland. First, there was a long-ranged look at the future of the Nation. This was necessary to fulfill the second phase of planning; to take advantage of opportunities to advance the projects. Next it was mandatory that the existing problems that must be solved be understood to complete the planned tasks. What became obvious was the plight of neglected children and the needs of families and the elderly. They all needed care, education, medical assistance, and some desperately needed a decent and safe place to live and grow. We saw many dysfunctional families and young people without purpose and decided the *"Anapausis mission"* was the answer.

When we first heard the word "Anapausis" and understood it to mean "refreshing" it caught our attention and we adopted it as a construct for the vision of bringing refreshment and happiness to others in our Homeland. The concept is an informal English transliteration of the Greek construct "anapsids" with use in the New Testament limited to Acts 3:19 normally translated as "refreshing" and another verb form used in 2 Timothy 1:16 for "refreshed." As with many Greek concepts the word has several meanings depending on the context. Consequently, the word was used to guide our thinking in building a home, the Anapausis Community; a

Conference Centre for the benefit of children, families, and faith-based groups, and scholarships for exceptional students, Bridge of Hope childcare facility, family life education services, Olive's House for eldercare, and O.A.S.I.S. University (***O****mega **A**dvance **S**chool for **I**nterdisciplinary **S**tudy*), a graduate program for the Caribbean.

Such aggressive planning could not be done alone and every advantage was taken to secure partners to advance the plans. The difficulty was getting bogged down in problem solving by failing to understand that many problems were solved by time and energy (money). Most strategic developers do not permit either time or money to hinder a worthy project. To get things done...things must be done! In strategic planning, problems that developed in a previous project were normally solved in planning the next endeavor; therefore, only when a project was nearing completion would dealing with new problems be considered. The goal was to use each opportunity to assist with solving the problems of the needy, but this would take time and funds and working partners would be needed to complete the vision as a collaborative enterprise.

Debbie and I saw a great need for passing on the basic lessons we had learned and the faith-based principles we were taught and beginning to practice. The task was great and we knew that we must have a clear vision of what was needed and a practical solution to solve these problems. It became clear that what was done for ourselves would die with us, but that a legacy could be constructed by what was done for others. In the process of developing and preserving a legacy several books were written; namely:

The Anapausis Partnership

--A Model of Philanthropy, Mentoring, and Coaching

ISBN: 978-1-935434-49-8

The book deals with common sense lessons and faith-based principles that result in a model of Philanthropy, Mentoring, and Coaching. It is a "How To" treatise on building both a relationship and advancing an agenda that benefits children, couples, faith-based groups, NGO'S, non-profit organizations, and family life. It is a true story of two individuals, who found each other amid their inspired mission to assist their homeland. It is a narrative of love and work, faith and worship, sacrament and service, stewardship and charity, teamwork and faithfulness. The pages are filled with common sense lessons that are later translated into faith-based principles and used to advance many projects for the benefit of the poor and needy.

God's Work Done God's Way

--You Don't Have to Make Headlines to Make a Difference

ISBN: 978-1-935434-60-3

Some see faith as a "vending machine," but the author shows not only the benefits of a faith-based life, but the obligations faith-based people use to accomplish their work with guidance from Providence. He believes that to live a life with purpose and significance will be a good life that benefits others. This book presents a lifestyle that cares for the disadvantaged and meets the challenge to get others involved. Quality thoughts and moral values come from believing and behaving learned principles. It is not what one gather, but what is scatter that defines the quality of life.

Living a Life Larger Than Yourself

ISBN: 978-1-935434-62-7

The word "happiness" as it is used today relies on the little word "hap" which means "good luck or by chance." Happenstance does not create a quality of life. Only purposeful behavior that is more than activities can bring the deep satisfaction of "happiness." Quality of life should not be confused with the standard of living, which is primarily income. The term "quality of life," as revealed in this book, is our positive intervention in the lives of the less fortunate.

Navigating the Challenges of Faith-based Behavior

--Conduct that Exhibits a Moral Course in Life

ISBN: 978-1-935434-64-1

A faith-based lifestyle determines both the course of action, the destination of the journey and provides a standard of behavior. Lifestyle provides intentionality of conduct and enables one to behave in a planned and deliberate way. The wise man Solomon was concerned about an empty life without permanent value that leads to frustration. He wrote, *"Pursue your course but know that God will judge your behavior."* (Ecclesiastes 11.9 EDOT) The value of a charted course relates to both the terminal objective and the time one has to travel toward stated goals. The design of this book illustrates in a nautical/sailing ship framework that there is a difference between *believe and behave.*

Ageing Has a Silver Lining

--Coping with Rainy Days

ISBN 978-1-935434-65-8

The purpose of the book is to improve the quality of life for seniors as they span the ageing process and move to their final decade of graceful ageing. The author deals with the difficulties of the ageing process, the senior living problems, the need for adequate eldercare facilities, and compassionate end of life care. The objective is to insure a Silver Lining to the clouds that surround the ageing process for seniors and their caregivers.

Adversity Leads to Achievement

--Learning to Surmount Difficulties

ISBN 978-1-935434-81-8

Adversity often becomes an open door of opportunity for achievement. Loss can actually create the opportunity for gain. This common sense lesson from the past is most telling, *"Necessity is the mother of invention."* Difficulties can become stumbling stones to produce present failure or stepping stones to a positive future.

The sale of these books support ongoing projects! Order from: *www.gea-books.com/bookstore/* or *subesh60@gmail.com* or anywhere good books are sold, including Amazon, Barnes and Noble, etc., and available on the Espresso Book Machine© in various venues.

Hopefully, planning would identify the weak and vulnerable spot for each project and make every effort to protect each project from such exposure. The adage of Achilles identifies the weakness of one of the great warriors of Greek mythology. According to legend, Achilles' mother wanted her son to be immortal, so she dipped the infant into the revered river Styx, believing the river's sacred waters would make him invincible. However, when dipping the boy in the river, her hand covered his heel, leaving it dry and unprotected. When Achilles went to fight in the Trojan War, an arrow struck the spot—his one weakness—and led to the hero's death. The good work of parents and past efforts do not always protect one from their individual weakness. The weak spots must be identified and protected for the arrows of misfortune. The best defense is a shield of faith and the presence of true friends who have ones best interest at heart.

Problems do not develop in a short space of time but

are normally the result of long standing neglect or failure to do something that was needed. Often it takes as long to solve a problem as it took to create the difficulty in the first place. Most individuals have multiple chances to do better or to correct bad behavior. What if we had only one chance to change, where would we be? There must be a tolerance and an understanding about human weakness and failure. Once this is clear it becomes easy to practice the Golden Rule *"Do unto others what you would have them do unto you."* Often we are hard on others when we see our own weaknesses expressed in their behavior. Memory of our own personal problems can make us more willing to assist those whose behavior is lacking in maturity. It takes time to grow a child, build a building, complete a project, or change a community. Patience becomes a virtue in dealing with such long-ranged difficulties. The practical words of the Golden Rule are expressed in most religions:

- **Buddhism** –"Hurt not others in ways that you yourself would find hurtful." (*Udana-Vaarga 5, 1*)

- **Christianity** –"As you would that men should do unto you, do you also to them likewise." (*Luke 6:31*)

- **Hinduism** – "This is the sum of duty; do naught unto others what you would not have them do unto you." (*Mahabharata 5, 1517*)

- **Judaism** – "What is hateful to you, do not do to your fellowman. This is the entire Law; all the rest is commentary." (*Talmud, Shabbat 3id*)

- **Taoism** – "Regard your neighbor's gain as your gain, and your neighbor's loss as your own loss." (*Tai Shang Kan Yin P'ien*)

Sacred writings are filled with individuals who had a

willingness but little else to fight moral and spiritual battles. David used his bare hands to kill a lion and a bear that tried to harm his father's sheep; he used a sling and one small stone to kill Goliath and a harp to soothe the raging soul of King Saul. Yes, David gathered five smooth stones from the brook, because Goliath was known to have four brothers. He was prepared. Shamgar had only an ox goad, and Samson used the jaw bone of a donkey to defeat a thousand Philistines. The young lad had only five loaves and two fishes, but the Master multiplied the food to feed thousands. Spiritual strength and personal talent are magnified to accomplish a divine purpose. What do you have to use against the enemies of the Cross? It may be small, but a willing heart is a large spiritual weapon against the force of evil. What can you do to improve the plight of children, families, and the elderly in your community or Nation?

When asked about my philosophy of change and how I take action when a door of opportunity is open for constructive social or moral change? First, I understand the energy and effort placed into existing programs that may not be fully meeting the present needs of individuals and groups involved. The next step is to understand that one should not "Throw out the baby with the bath water!" All working elements and useable people of a corporate or organizational operation should be preserved with respect to those who have previously labored in the same vineyard or on the program or project. Then bold and swift action is required to accomplish any worthy project. One should always remember, "The end is worth the journey!"

The same is true when working with individuals. One must look at and pay attention to the parents and family that brought the person to where they presently find themselves.

Parents and families are not perfect, because they are human. However, there is no human problem or difficulty that divinely guided intervention cannot improve the situation or solve the problem. Social and spiritual change moves slowly, and all who would make a difference in groups or with individuals must be patient and understand the slow and constant nature of change.

Change is the one constant in life; however, all change is not positive. Change is the current flowing stream on which the circumstances of life are altered for the better with adequate guidance and sincere effort. To assure that changes in services, programs, and projects are positive, one needs a clear model for constructive change. Change in institutions, organizations, and groups are normally slower than changes in most individuals. At times there is a divine interruption in one's life that produces drastic change. Normally, change is gradual and occurs over time, and to be positive change, guidance and direction by others is normally required. This constant effort toward positive change can create a seamless process that is smooth and constructive.

The Great Wall of China was built over several generations to protect the country from foreign invaders. Many years and many lives were the price of constructing the wall. In fact many workers who died on the job were buried as part of the wall itself to honor their commitment to protect their country from invaders. During many dynasties and decades the wall has stood as a symbol of concern for the safety of their country. The wall was never breached by foreign invaders, but China was invaded many times, not by breaching the wall, but by bribing the keepers of the gates.

When all the wall of Jerusalem was completed except one gate, the enemy attempted to stop the work and leave one gate open as an easy entrance. Nehemiah, however, would not come down from the wall; he would not stop the work; and he would not go into the plain of Ono to meet with the enemy. Each time he said, *"OH NO, this good work will not be stopped until it is finished!"* Nehemiah intended to complete the wall and secure the gates. He understood that the wall not only needed gates, but strong keepers of the gates. Nehemiah was a strong leader and was able to maintain courage and participation until the work was finished. Weak leadership normally causes discouragement among the rank and file of workers and limits their social connectedness. As the influence of a leader decreases, the quality and strength of the association is limited.

God works through faith-based people to accomplish seemingly impossible tasks. Providence and parents shape individuals with gifts, talents, personality characteristics, experience and training to prepare them for a Divine Mission the extent of which most do not readily understand what is in store for them.

It appears from sacred writings that God prepared and positioned Nehemiah to accomplish an almost impossible task recorded in scripture. By obedient faith, Nehemiah was able to overcome what appeared to be great opposition and insurmountable distractions. His fervent prayer was generally short, *"Oh, God strengthen my hands"* (Nehemiah 6:9). God calls us to be available and faithful, not to *be successful*. *Success suggests* "more than enough" and no one doing God's work can do more than is required. "...when you have done all those things commanded of you, say, We are unprofitable servants we have done that which was our duty." (Luke 17:10 EDNT)

LEARNING TO SURMOUNT DIFFICULTIES

Start by doing what is necessary, then, what is possible, and suddenly you are doing the impossible.

– St. Francis of Assisi

ADVERSITY LEADS TO ACHIEVEMENT

Many of life's failures come when people did not realize how close they were to success when they gave up.

–Thomas Edison

10

WEAK LEADERSHIP BREEDS DISCOURAGEMENT

The ability to influence others is a primary role of leaders regardless of their place in society: parent, professor, politician, policeman, pastor, friends, or members of the extended family. When influence is weakened others become discouraged. Negative behavior of influential people impacts all who follow them. When an individual behaves in a negative manner in a relationship, the ability to influence others to voluntarily follow in the desired direction is thwarted. Cooperation in completing a plan, reaching a goal, or solving a problem is weakened and at times completely broken. Inspiration is the difference between feeling self-reliant and being overwhelmed or frightened about present circumstance or the foreseeable future.

Inspiration is akin to encouragement. Some believe that perception is reality; that is, the way one actually feels about their existence. The way individuals feel about themselves has an enormous impact on how they are identified by others. When the confidence is low, the self-assurance will be low. This will cause others to view an individual as being insecure. This view causes family or friends to view someone as unproductive. With this attitude the sky is always filled with dark clouds and uncertainty. When the factors that affect self-confidence bring a loss of influence, family, friends, and coworkers should encourage the things that improve self-confidence. This will bring an element of inspiration to the current situation.

Individuals are used to solve social problems and make a difference in the lives of others. The specialized talents of one person can make a difference in the circumstance of others and in society. This means individuals reaching their own family, their friends, their colleagues at work, their neighbor in the community, and even their enemies. God uses the personal talents and personality of individuals to change the world. This sacrificial service is great, but obedience is what produces such sacrifice. A young missionary killed by natives wrote in his journal, *"A man is no fool who gives up what he cannot keep to gain what he cannot lose."* To give up something you prefer for something God values is the essence of sacrifice. To submit to a call and to listen and pay attention to a spiritual duty is conformity to God's will. What is done for personal advantage dies with the person, but what is accomplished for others becomes both a well-spoken eulogy and a moral legacy.

> *8. Finally, you must think the same thoughts, suffer with one another, having automatic interdependence with brotherly kindness; be tender-hearted and humble-minded: 9. you must not repay injury with injury, or hard words with hard words, but bless those who curse you. For you were called to give kind words to others and come to a well-spoken eulogy at the end. 10. For the one wishing to love life and see prosperous days, let him avoid an evil tongue and cunning words. 11. Habitually avoid evil, and do good things; let him seek and follow peace.*
>
> -- (1 Peter 3:8-11 EDNT)

It is normal to experience *"growing pains"* as a part of the maturing process and progress in life and career. Some think they can simply practice the same old stuff day after day and that persistence alone will produce progress or success. This is a tragic fault of many who fail in their endeavors. There must be consistent effort, but also planning and the use of common sense is required. Keeping a journal of activities can assist in producing variety into a project and assist in understanding areas of weakness that hinder progress. This means change. One must develop an entrepreneur spirit, become creative and take the risk. Caution! All ventures into new areas carry an element of risk. There are hazards in most undertakings. A wrong move could cause a human setback in the process of assisting others. This is why one must take *"pains"* to do it right. Starting over is a hard thing to do. There is an old saying, *"Why is there never enough time to do it right, but always sufficient time to do it over?"*

When Nehemiah arrived in Jerusalem, he went secretly at night and surveyed the situation and determined what had to be done. Then he said to the people, *"Come let us build up the wall of Jerusalem that we no more be criticized for doing something wrong."* When the people heard that the King had given permission and was to furnish the timber they said, *"Let us rise up and build."* And their hands were strengthened for the task at hand. When criticism came, Nehemiah said,

> *"The God of heaven will prosper us and His servants will rise up and build; but you who do not participate will have no portion, nor right, nor memorial in this place."*

And the people worked side-by-side to repair the wall and the gates of the city. Then the enemy grew angry because the wall and the gates were being rebuilt. There developed a conspiracy among the enemies to hinder the work on the wall. When the people stood up to the enemies they divided the work: half worked on the wall and half held a weapon. Then to assure a timely completion of the project each worker worked with one hand and with the other held a weapon. As they were scattered in various places working on the wall, when the enemy attacked one place, they sounded the trumpet and all the workers converged on that place to protect the work. When the enemy came strong and hid among the rubbish, Nehemiah told the people, *"Let everyone lodge in the city until the work is done."* In other words, stay at the job site until the work is finished.

There will always be opposition to moral and ethical work. Not only is work for faith-based groups understood to be good work, but the work to supply the needs of the poor is divine work. Opposition continued, and the people were about to rebel at Nehemiah's work rules because of lost wages from working on the wall. Nehemiah said, *"We will restore all you have lost. Do not worry, God is in control."* Nehemiah fed all the people at his table, and God blessed the work. It is clear that no one will lose when they work to rebuild what the enemy has torn down. Not only to rebuild, but the effort should be to build strong enough that an enemy cannot again tear the structure down.

Building strong relationships or structuring a good business organization is similar to the concept of wellness in health issues. The notion of wellness is generally used to express a positive approach to a healthy balance of body, mind, and spirit or the essence of the life-force that brings a sense of well-being. Everything related to wellness is a result of a deliberate effort to remain viable and function as a healthy person. When one does not or cannot manage the issues of health, there is a loss of functional efficiency and the sense of well-being is gradually diminished until it overtakes the issue of physical health.

ADVERSITY LEADS TO ACHIEVEMENT

Wellness is a state of full mental, physical, and social well-being, — not merely the absence of disease or infirmity.

11

UNDERSTANDING FACILITATES WELLNESS AND HEALTH

Health and wellness is more than two sides of the same coin. Wellness determines health; health pre-supposes wellness. The World Health Organization explained *"Wellness is the optimal state of health."* Health has to do with fitness, strength and the general physical condition. When one feels ill, sick, or ailing, they are in discomfort or have *dis-ease*. One sees a medical professional and is given medicine to mask the symptoms until the *dis-ease* goes away. Meanwhile, the sick person becomes a *"patient"* meaning *"they remain under the pressure of the disease or complaint until an adequate remedy is found."*

Often the malady called illness is brought on by personal behavior, eating or drinking the wrong stuff, poor sleeping habits, little exercise, and sometimes something as simple as drinking insufficient amounts of water on a daily basis. However, the illness we call disease may simply be an interruption of the normal routine of life and is a *"wake-up call"* that something about life and living needs to be changed.

Here again difficulties create opportunity for a person to make the necessary adjustments in lifestyle to regain their health.

Wellness is a state of full mental, physical, and social well-being, and not merely the absence of disease or infirmity. The National Wellness Institute (USA) defined wellness as *"a conscious, self-directed and evolving process of achieving full potential."* When one does not or cannot manage health issues, there is the loss of functional efficiency and the sense of well-being is gradually diminished until it overtakes the issue of health. Physical health is generally influenced by job satisfaction and performance, personal social relations with friends, family, and workplace acquaintance, and overall happiness and satisfaction with one's lot and station in life.

As a young student in my village, teachers from the Presbyterian School began sowing seeds of truth from sacred scripture into my life. At age 23 and during a serious illness I was hospitalized with a failing kidney. An Adventist Hospital Chaplain came to my room and read from the Sacred Book words of encouragement that gave me hope in the midst of despair. Although I was aware of sacred writings, I had never been this close to death and had never listened with the same intensity as I did from a sick bed. A small spiritual seed was planted in my life that would flourish later. The medical treatments were failing to solve the problem and there had to be additional intervention. A kidney ailment brought me near death during my early employment. The Adventist Chaplain read words of encouragement from the Bible and this gave me hope that I would live provided the additional interventions were available.

Good and bad change often comes slowly in life. In some cases there is drastic change in lifestyle and behavior, but in others a seed is planted, watered, and cultivated, before it comes to positive or negative fruition. It appears that this is the way moral matters enter daily life. The seeds of truth were planted deep in my subconscious, but it took my illness with kidney failure to water that seed and open my eyes to see how Providence used the illness, family, doctors and hospital staff to get my attention directed toward the value of life and the future. Serious illness is one way God got my attention and helped me see my need to change and to value partnering with others to make life more effective. Realization that life was about the future, not present difficulties, illness, or troubles, was a positive eye-opener. Letting Providence and circumstances take a constructive hold on me literally turned my life around.

Looking back on my life, I can see how God used my illness, my family, my teachers, and good medical services to spare my life for His purpose. Although I did not understand these facts at the time, the process was teaching me that a Higher Power was intervening in my life. When the medical treatment in Trinidad failed to produce recovery and the health issues became more complicated, I was transported to Canada for additional life-saving treatment. With no medical insurance the concern was how could a gravely ill village boy find the resources for life-saving medical treatment in a foreign country? Problems in life always present God an opportunity to intervene.

Providentially, a door of opportunity was opened and life began to have more grace and value. Thankfully, the maturity was there to walk (or in this case) be carried through that door. God does not only work on the person who is sick, but intervenes in others to get involved and become part of the solution. God's solution normally requires human participation and obedience.

My father sold a piece of property for my airfare to Canada. My older brother placed me on his Canadian Blue Cross/Blue Shield Insurance policy, and an uncle who was a Canadian Physician arranged and supervised my treatment. Looking back it is easy to see how Providence planned to care for me. God was getting my attention as a crucially ill young man. The watering of the seed of truth was in full operation. God was working and the watered seed was sprouting. Normally one who is dangerously ill and facing death would begin to look to a Higher Power for assistance, especially when family, friends, and the medical staff had done all they could do. This is what happened to me. When I was lost, God found me and was caring for me and preparing me for a mission in my homeland. I was learning more about family and divine intervention. Wellness and good health were becoming part of my daily thinking and lifestyle.

After an operation to remove the diseased kidney, I was welcomed into my uncle's home in Canada for a recovery period before returning to Trinidad. When I did return my dream of owning my own business was uppermost in my mind. My life had been spared for a purpose. These opportunities for learning and work in the business arena of Port of Spain further enhanced my experience and allowed me to develop as a person. This growth and development increased my desire to own my own business. Companies such as the Bata Shoe Company, Ltd. and my teacher in academic O-Levels, including one in the Principles of Business and Accounting, probably never realized that God used them to prepare me for the adventure in business experienced later in my life.

Exactly what that purpose was to be was not completely known to me. I knew what I wanted to do, but the real issue was where to start and who is going to assist with the effort. So it was decided to start in Trinidad where my family roots were. Surely out of seven brothers at least one would be willing to assist with new business ventures in Trinidad. The only thing I knew was hard work so I put my mind and limited resources into starting the House of Marketing, Ltd. a business that still flourishes today and assists with funding support for the vision of the *Anapausis Partnership* that built the Anapausis Community, and several other charitable projects.

My workaholic mindset drove me to work hard to generate resources. I was determined to make my businesses work. However, this compulsive need to work hard for long hours took a toll on my health and my family life. I decided to take my children to Miami for schooling while I traveled back and forth between Trinidad and the United States. I had an upscale home in Miami Lakes, Florida with a beautifully landscaped backyard and a pool, but something was missing in my life. God was permitting human circumstances beyond my complete control to alter my life and future. I learned later that God does not waste a hurt, but with each and every difficulty brings a way forward. Each crisis in life is both a danger and an opportunity. A danger that I would become negative and miss the opportunity was a real possibility, but my better angels prevailed and I began to consider spiritual matters.

When my children joined me from Trinidad things began to change for the better. The needs of growing children bring out the best in parents. My daughter was enrolled in a Day School operated by a local church and we began attending Sunday services and encountered people with a joyful attitude. God was working in my life and enabling me to plan for a prosperous lifestyle and become a good steward of time, resources, and relationships.

Henry Ford coined the phrase: "If you think you can, or think you can't... you're right!"

12

PLANNING ENSURES A PROSPEROUS LIFESTYLE

Rich or poor, God expects everyone to be good stewards of the accumulated assets acquired over time. This is stewardship and for faith-based people this word carries special and complex meaning. Not only do faith-based people tithe to support their place of worship, they also tithe their time, talent, and energy assisting the less fortunate. Through mentoring and coaching, some develop a model of philanthropy. A goal of all social, business, and spiritual endeavors is to create a reproducible model of support, benefaction, investment, sponsorship, accountability, and direct and indirect aid to the needy.

My desire was to express generosity in a socially responsible way and to raise benevolence to a more spiritual level that created a greater sensitivity to basic human needs. Helping others was both direct and indirect in a manner that was soft and sincere to improve the general welfare of those in need. To do this required a great deal of mentoring of individuals in the form of advising, coaching, counseling, guiding, teaching by example, and direct tutoring. This was done to reproduce common sense lessons and translate them into faith-based principles that could change the attitudes and practices of others.

Tragically, some let bitterness or an unconcerned attitude keep them from becoming usable in the hand of God. Most mothers pass moral principles on to their children. Some of these statements are remembered and become both an anchor and a guide for life. People who will not help themselves will never be prepared for a productive work with others. Give hungry people food and they will be back tomorrow for more. Teach them how to grow a garden and they can eventually feed themselves and their families. If they are willing to plant a garden or take a job, assist them only until the first paycheck or the garden produces food. Should they be unwilling to make the effort, provide your assistance where it will be appreciated, in other words, all charity must be done with care and due diligence to be certain that those being assisted are worthy of the support and concern.

Henry Ford coined the phrase: *"If you think you can, or think you can't - you're right!"* This means that by thinking positively, the brain will create the circumstances that produce achievement. The concept is simple. By maintaining a positive attitude, others will dress the part, look the part, say the right thing at the right time, and generally be attractive to the people around them. No one wants to be around negative people. Positive thinking is a basic ingredient of worthwhile progress. Negativity of leaders produces distrust, doubt and suspicion which weaken their influence.

If a rotten apple can spoil a whole basket of fruit, what can *"bad apples"* in the home and community produce? Just look around at the crime ridden communities filled with dysfunctional families and blinded observers who look the other way to avoid involvement in the tragic scenes. When the blind lead, all the people end up in the ditch of despair and depression with a hopeless feeling deep within their internal organs. A simple change in the spiritual aspects of the situation can produce good seed and assure a better community and family harvest in the future. Bad apples must be removed to limit their negative influence on the children and the community. Weak and timid souls are hindered in their planning for a prosperous future and moral lifestyle.

During troubled times people usually are willing to lay aside differences and join the effort to remove the cause of the conflict. These are perilous times of poverty and crime. A small group of people are willing to become involved and a few organizations have agreed to work with them to attack the issues of poverty. The less fortunate and the poor cannot lift themselves out of the clutches of poverty. However, there is sufficient wealth and available energy and programs provided the compassion can be turned into commitment and the commitment transformed into concerted activity and workable programs. The poor do not need a hand out; they need and want a hand up. Normally the poor lack opportunity and need someone to provide a hand. This is the only way they will stand tall and become a productive citizen of the community. Although some are *"just takers"* the opportunity to assist the willing is a chance worth the effort.

Just as any conflict or battle with opposition forces, it may not be possible to win the battle against poverty immediately and some remedial and tutorial work will be required to assist the disadvantaged children and dysfunctional families toward a positive and productive lifestyle. If we can win their heart and soul, they will work with us in a long-term project. Gradually the poor and needy will boost themselves into a better quality life and begin to develop improved circumstances for their family.

The developing model included a great deal of team-type and personal coaching that incorporated hands-on experience and personal guidance as to how some things could be done differently; how other things could be done better, and how new things could be done that would solve personal, family and community problems and improve the quality of life for those involved. A model is of little value unless it is understood and reproduced. The reader should review the lessons and the faith-based principles learned from others and after careful consideration, take the nectar from those that are meaningful and make their own honey. Review your own life-lessons and develop your principles into a model of stewardship and generous benevolence. This could make a difference in the needs of your community.

A principle established at Creation was *"the seed is in the fruit,"* (Genesis 1:11). Each living thing reproduces itself with all the same essential elements and features. Each element of God's Creation reproduced itself from the basic DNA (deoxyribonucleic acid), an essential component of all living matter, and the basic material in a cell that transmits the hereditary pattern. Bad parents, bad siblings, bad leaders, bad citizens, and the list increases over time. Every bad influence reproduces and perpetuates itself. Even good seed in a bad environment will produce a weak plant that is normally short lived. Sacred writings are clear that *"the fruit of a bitter root," may* corrupt many. The fact is that Esau, who sold his birthright for a bowl of soup, changed the future of succeeding generations. A prosperous future requires careful planning to avoid any cause for animosity.

> *14. Pursue harmony with all men, and strive for that consecration without which no man shall see the Lord: 15. Watch that no one misses the grace of God; lest any cause for animosity grow up to trouble you, and thereby many be corrupted; 16. Watch that no one falls into sexual impurity or follows a blasphemous person, as Esau, who for a scrap of food gave up the rights of the first born. 17. Afterward, he was eager enough to have the blood related honor, but was rejected: he had no opportunity to change his mind, although he sought that blessing with tears.*
>
> (Hebrews 12:14-17 EDNT)

It becomes clearer each day as one reads the daily newspaper or listens to the 24/7 news that families and communities are in deep trouble. Even the financially prudent economies of Nations are reaping the harvest of bad seeds from past extravagances of careless generations. This trouble comes from *"bad seeds"* and from the *"bitter roots"* caused by neglect, abandonment, and abuse that are prevalent in society. The sad part is that it was preventable by capable individuals, faith-based groups, and Government entities, but those able to restrain corruption that results in bad parents and incomplete and dysfunctional families are doing little if anything to prevent or rectify the situation. Where others fail, faith-based groups should be able to network and access the material and spiritual provisions provided by Providence to deal with moral aspects of the problem. It takes planning, money, and energy to produce positive social and spiritual change in a community. The worse it gets the more energy and effort it takes to change the progressive decline of morality and related behavior. The ethical issue is to act immediately with workable programs to deal with the dysfunction. Delay could be disastrous for all concerned.

God is no respecter of persons; each human being is loved the same. I am confident as God dealt with me many years ago, divine authority can and will deal with others to search for ways and means to make a difference. It may not be just the same way God worked with me, because each individual is different, and God works within the framework of each individual's life and capability. Pray, earnestly desire the true faith of the early believers, read and study the sacred writings, and you will receive a clear understanding of exactly what God wants you to do and how you can become involved more effectively in working for positive social change.

You may never be listed in a book of great accomplishments. Just remember you do not have to make headlines to make a difference in the lives of those around you. You may feel that little has been accomplished, but others see a different picture of you. Remember Joseph. He is considered by most scholars as a type of the Deliverer; however, he was not included in the Chapter of Heroes (Hebrews 13) although he resisted the advances of Potiphar's wife, saved his family from starvation, saved the Land of Egypt following a great drought, or for his forgiving spirit in dealing with his brothers who sold him into slavery. Yet he was listed in the Faith Chapter (Hebrews 11) because he claimed his part of the Divine Promise. God had promised to deliver His People from Egyptian bondage and return them to the land of their fathers. Joseph claimed his part of the promise.

When Israel left Egypt they took Joseph's bones and buried them in a plot prepared by his father. Genesis begins with God's creation of the heavens and earth and ends with a coffin in Egypt, (Genesis 50:26). A coffin and honors in Egypt were not the end of Joseph's story. Joseph's claim to fame in Hebrews was that he believed in Divine Promises and claimed his place in the Promise Land. Joseph overcame sibling rivalry, lies that put him in prison, but turned adversity into achievement. He developed a prosperous lifestyle for himself, his family, and the land of Egypt. Joseph had a well-spoken eulogy at the end. The Book of Genesis begins with the Creation of all things, including man, and ends with a coffin in Egypt, but the faith of Joseph turned the "coffin in Egypt" into a victorious journey back to a place provided for him by his father.

> *By faith Joseph when he came to the end of his life, spoke of the departing of Israel from Egypt, and gave orders for the removal of his bones,*
>
> (Hebrews 11:22 EDNT).

God, the Heavenly Father of us all, has provided a place for all of us. Joseph overcame the adversities of life and became a moral citizen of Egypt and by claiming God's Promise, became a mystical citizen of Heaven. Will you have a well-spoken eulogy at the end of your life? Have you claimed your part of God's Promise?

> *8. Finally, you must think the same thoughts, suffer with one another, having automatic interdependence with brotherly kindness; be tender-hearted and humble-minded: 9. you must not repay injury with injury, or hard words with hard words, but bless those who curse you. For you were called to give kind words to others and come to a well-spoken eulogy at the end. 10. For the one wishing to love life and see prosperous days, let him avoid an evil tongue and cunning words. 11. Habitually avoid evil, and do good things; let him seek and follow peace.*
>
> -- (1 Peter 3:8-11 EDNT)

ADVERSITY LEADS TO ACHIEVEMENT

> To find your mission in life is to discover the intersection between your greatest desire and the world's greatest hunger.
>
> —Frederick Buechner

ABOUT THE AUTHOR

Subesh Ramjattan is a remarkable man who is hungry for knowledge and reaches for every kernel of truth he can find from any source. His life journey began in a poor village learning common sense lessons from his family and the village environment. He proceeded to learn more in school and as a young man working hard to gather both the knowledge and the resources needed to start his own business. He listens to anyone who speaks and reads every-thing in sight. Subesh remembers almost everything good he hears, sees, or learns from any source. He is unselfish in giving resources for projects for the disadvantaged and constantly demonstrates his concern for faith-based operations and the individuals who take an active role in faith-based groups.

Subesh is a serious student of all subjects that touch his life, business and spiritual reality. When he discovers the interrelationship of concepts and constructs, he desires to share them with others. This interest has resulted in a business and spiritual journey that has increased the quality of life for many. His first book, *The Anapausis Partnership*, co-authored with his wife, Debra, catalogued much of the business and spiritual journey that established a model of philanthropy, mentoring, and coaching to improve the quality of life for the disadvantaged of Trinidad and Tobago. The documentation of this process produced the awarding of a Doctor of Humane Letters (DHL) by OASIS University's Institute of Higher

Learning (2010). In 2015, the University of the West Indies (UWI) recognized the contribution Dr. Ramjattan had made to the literature and the people of Trinidad and Tobago based on his first five books and his philanthropy with the awarding of the Doctor of Letters (DLitt).

Dr. Ramjattan's latest book, *Adversity Leads to Achievement: Learning to Surmount Difficulties,* is a guide to deal with difficulties and keep focused on the present mission. To accomplish this, one must both define and refine personal values to provide clear thinking when trouble comes. Establish goals and keep in mind that everything that happens is about the future; consequently, do not dwell on the problem but see how the solution could benefit your future and assist others. Maintain confidence in yourself and your mission. Keep your trust in those around you and accept their assistance. Always put your personal pride on the back burner and provide a model of resilience in the face of difficulties. Maintain true spirituality and keep a sense of humor, and others will voluntarily follow you toward your stated goals. This is where adversity leads to achievement.

All of Dr. Ramjattan's books may be purchased from gea-books.com/bookstore/author's page or amazon.com, barnesandnoble.com and the Espresso Book Machine© or anywhere good books are sold.

Proceeds from Dr. Ramjattan's books support ongoing projects.

AFTERWORD

Subesh Ramjattan

Classic literature on adversity and leadership suggests that personal growth and character *"create the climate in which people turn challenging opportunities into remarkable successes."* (Kouses and Posner (2003). As I look back over my life and career, I see both adversity and achievement. My parents were born to hard times. For me, growing up was problematic, education was difficult, leaving home was traumatic, health was distressing, and work experience was both challenging and rewarding. I was able at age 23 to take what my parents taught me and what I learned in school and work experience and start my own business: The House of Marketing, Ltd. in Trinidad. This is why I decided to share some thoughts about Adversity Leads to Achievement.

Don't get me wrong, life was good, too! I was surprised that so many assisted me on my quest for learning, search for spiritual matters, and patience with me as I learned on the job. This book was written as a source of encouragement to others who may be encountering the normal difficulties and disappointments of life. They will surely come and at times they seem to pile on, one after another. Always remember that whatever comes your way, God meant it for good. Never become discouraged; make the most of each opportunity to move forward.

When difficulties come you will remember the old saying, that *"Trouble comes in three(s)!"* Then you will spend days looking for more trouble or waiting for the other shoe to drop. My advice is clear, do not wait for more trouble, but deal with the present issue as quickly as possible. Difficult situations must never be allowed to fester and get worse. However, life is not all bad, because there are redeeming virtues in most people and in many hardships.

The famous English writer, C. S. Lewis once wrote *"Hardships often prepare ordinary people for an extraordinary destiny."* So when trouble comes, thank God for the opportunity to learn, grow, mature, and achieve. Rejoice because you have a choice of a new direction. Note the words of James in sacred writing:

> *2. My cherished band of believers, count it a jewel (precious stone) when you fall into adversity and testing that gives a choice of direction.*
>
> (James 1:2 EDNT)

Generally, adversity is unexpected and is always disruptive with a degree of uncertainty as to the path through it or the outcome of the effort. Achievement is a realization of value added when difficulties are overcome. This may appear to be an absurdity of achievement, but there is never gain without pain. Rejoice because you have a choice; instead of, just maintaining the *status quo*.

In the Hebrew sacred writings, the concept of adversity is presented in terms of distress and evil expressed in four Hebrew words meaning, *(1)* "a halting," or "fall,"; *(2)* "passages or channels," "distress," or "affliction,";*(3)* "narrow channel," or "affliction,"; *(4)* "bad," "evil," or "harmful." These various forms cover the misfortunes caused by enemies, poverty, sorrow, and trouble. Adversity occurs only once in the Greek sacred writings as *"ill-treated"* or *"ill-treatment."*

> 3. Remember those who are in prison for you yourselves know what it is like to be a prisoner; remember those who are suffering ill-treatment for the same thing can happen to you so long as you are in the body.
>
> (Hebrews 13:3 EDNT)

Many see adversity as an unwelcome disruption in their life and work, yet adversity is both purifying and sustaining to those who perservere in solving the antecedent cause and profit from the solution. It becomes clear that adversity is unavoidable in most situations in life. Sacred writings explained *"man that is born of woman is of few days and full of trouble."* Consequently, one must develop a strategy to deal with adversaries and obstacles in the pathway to achievement.

The question is not *"Will you face difficulties, but when will they come and how will you deal with problem times?"* One deals with adversities from both an internal and external perspective. The internal strength comes from the way you see the world, your predisposition to behave in a certain way, and the depth of your personal grounding and spirituality. External strategies to deal with adversity come primarily from your connectedness with family, friends, and stakeholders. Always accept assistance, because *"A burden is lighter when shared."* Adversity reveals true friends and at times new friends. Achievements shared with participants become a blessing to all.

To overcome difficulties and keep focused on the present mission, one must both define and refine personal values to provide clear thinking when trouble comes. Establish goals and keep in mind that everything that happens is about the future; consequently, do not dwell on the problem but see how the solution could benefit your future and assist others. Maintain confidence in yourself and your mission. Keep your trust in those around you and accept their assistance. Always put your personal pride on the back burner and provide a model of resilience in the face of difficulties. Maintain true spirituality and keep a sense of humor, and others will voluntarily follow you toward your stated goals. This is where adversity leads to achievement.

> *8. Never be embarrassed for the witness (lifestyle) you give of our Lord, nor of me his prisoner: but be a participant in the sufferings of the gospel according to the power of God; 9. Who saved us and called us with a call to consecration, not according to our achievements, but according to His own purpose and grace, before the world began, 10. But is now made clear by the appearing of our Savior Jesus Christ, who hath abolished death, and hath brought life and immortality to light through the gospel:*
>
> (2 Timothy 1:8-10 EDNT)

RESOURCE BIBLIOGRAPHY

Berry, W. (2007). The Uses of Adversity. *Sewanee Review*, *115*(2), 211–238.

Bolden, R., & Kirk, P. (2009). African Leadership: Surfacing New Understandings through Leadership Development. *International Journal of Cross Cultural Management, 9*(1), 69–86.

Durkin, J., & Joseph, S. (2009). Growth Following Adversity and Its Relation with Subjective Well-Being and Psychological Well-Being. *Journal of Loss and Trauma, 14*(3), 228–234.

Farmer, T. A., & Officer, C. (2010). Overcoming adversity: resilience development strategies for educational leaders. *Health (San Francisco)*, (2005).

Galli, N., & Vealey, R. S. (2008). "Bouncing Back" From Adversity : Athletes' Experiences of Resilience. *Kinesiology*, (2002), 316–335.

Green, Hollis L. (2013). *Fighting the Amalekites: A Guide to Spiritual Warfare*. Nashville. gea-books.

Jackson, D., Frito, A., & Edenborough, M. (2007). Personal resilience as a strategy for surviving and thriving in the face of workplace adversity: a literature review. *Journal of advanced nursing, 60*(1), 1–9.

Kouzes, J., and Posner, B., (2003). *The Leadership Challenge*. Wiley.

Lee, T., Kwong, W., Cheung, C., Ungar, M., & Cheung, M. Y. L. (2009). Children's Resilience-Related Beliefs as a Predictor of Positive Child Development in the Face of Adversities: Implications for Interventions to Enhance Children's Quality of Life. *Social Indicators Research, 95*(3), 437–453.

Levenson, A. R. (2002). Leveraging Adversity for Strategic Advantage. *Science, 31*(2), 165–176.

Moore, Christian (2014).*The Resilience Breakthrough: 27 Tools for Turning Adversity into Action*. Greenleaf Books Group.

Stanley, Charles (2002). *How to Handle Adversity*. Thomas Nelson.

Southwick S. M., Litz B. T., Charney D. S. and Friedman M. J. (2011) *Resilience and Mental Health: Challenges Across the Lifespan.* Cambridge: Cambridge University Press.

Stoltz, P. (1997). *Adversity quotient: Turning obstacles into opportunities.* New York: Wiley.

Stoltz, P. (2001). *Adversity Quotient at Work: Finding Your Hidden Capacity for Getting Things Done.* Collins.

Stoner, C., & Gilligan, J. (2002). Leader rebound: how successful managers bounce back from the tests of adversity. *Business Horizons, 45*(6), 17–24.

Wilson, M., & Rice, S. S. (2004). Wired to Inspire Leading Organizations Through Adversity. *Leadership in Action, 24*(2), 3–8.

Ungar M. (2012). *The Social Ecology of Resilience: A Handbook of Theory and Practice.* New York: Springer Science.

APPENDIX A:
Adversity Response Profile (ARP)

To create your **Adversity Response Profile (ARP),** imagine the following events as if they were happening right now. Then circle the number that represents your answer to each of the related questions.

1. You suffer a financial setback. *To what extent can you influence this situation?*

    Not at all **1 2 3 4 5** Completely

2. You are overlooked for a promotion. *To what extent do you feel responsible for improving the situation?*

    Not responsible at all **1 2 3 4 5** Completely responsible

3. You are criticized for a big project that you just completed. *The consequences of this situation will:*

Affect all aspects of my life **1 2 3 4 5** Be limited to this situation

4. You accidentally delete an important email. *The consequences of this situation will:*

    Last forever **1 2 3 4 5** Quickly pass

5. The high-priority project you are working on gets canceled. *The consequences of this situation will:*

Affect all aspects of my life **1 2 3 4 5** Be limited to this situation

6. Someone you respect ignores your attempt to discuss an important issue. *To what extent do you feel responsible for improving this situation?*

Not responsible at all **1 2** 3 **4 5** Completely responsible

7. People respond unfavorably to your latest ideas. *To what extent can you influence this situation?*

Not at all **1 2 3 4 5** Completely

8. You are unable to take a much-needed vacation. *The consequences of this situation will:*

Last forever **1 2 3 4 5** Quickly pass

9. You hit every red light on your way to an important appointment. *The consequences of this situation will:*

Affect all aspects of my life **1 2 3 4 5** Be limited to this situation

10. After extensive searching, you cannot find an important document. *The consequences of this situation will:*

Last forever **1 2 3 4 5** Quickly pass

11. Your workplace is understaffed. *To what extent do you feel responsible for improving this situation?*

Not responsible at all **1 2 3 4 5** Completely responsible

12. You miss an important appointment. *The consequences of this situation will:*

Affect all aspects of my life **1 2 3 4 5** Be limited to this situation

13. Your personal and work obligations are out of balance. *To what extent can you influence this situation?*

Not at all **1 2 3 4 5** Completely

14. You never seem to have enough money. *The consequences of this situation will:*

Last forever **1 2 3 4 5** Quickly pass

15. You do not exercise regularly though you know you should. *To what extent can you influence this situation?*

Not at all **1 2 3 4 5** Completely

16. Your organization is not meeting its goals. *To what extent do you feel responsible for improving this situation?*

Not responsible at all **1 2 3 4 5** Completely responsible

17. Your computer crashed for the third time this week. *To what extent can you influence this situation?*

Not at all **1 2 3 4 5** Completely

18. The meeting you are in is mostly a waste. *To what extent do you feel responsible for improving this situation?*

Not responsible at all **1 2 3 4 5** Completely responsible

19. You lost something that is important to you. *The consequences of this situation will:*

Last forever **1 2 3 4 5** Quickly pass

20. **Your boss adamantly disagrees with your decision.** *The consequences of this situation will:*

Affect all aspects of my life **1 2 3 4 5** Be limited to this situation

©2006 Winston J. Brill & Associates.
All rights reserved.

[See AQ scoring PLAN APPENDIX B]

APPENDIX B: Scoring: ADVERSITY QUOTIENT (AQ)

Your **AQ** response is comprised of four **CORE** dimensions. Understanding these four is the first step toward improving your response to adversity, expanding your capacity, and, ultimately, increasing your overall **AQ**.

Insert each of the 20 numbers you circled in Appendix A *Adversity Response Profile (ARP)* next to the corresponding number below. Then insert the total for each column. Add the four totals and multiply that number by two for your final score.

<u>C</u>	<u>O</u>	<u>R</u>	<u>E</u>
1. ___	2. ___	3. ___	4. ___
7. ___	6. ___	5. ___	8. ___
13. ___	11. ___	9. ___	10. ___
15. ___	16. ___	12. ___	14. ___
17. ___	18. ___	20. ___	19. ___
Total C ___	Total O ___	Total R ___	Total E ___

Total C+O+R+E = _____ x 2 = ARP Score = _____

The average ARP score is 147.5. What's your score? The higher the better.

Now, look at your **CORE** breakdown and determine which aspects of the AQ you need to improve.

C = Control

To what extent can you influence the situation?

How much control do you perceive you have?

Those with higher AQs perceive they have significantly more control and influence in adverse situations than do those with lower AQs. Even in situations that appear overwhelming or out of their hands, those with higher AQs find some facet of the situation they can influence. Those with lower AQs respond as if they have little or no control and often give up.

O = Ownership

To what extent do you hold yourself responsible for improving this situation?

To what extent are you accountable to play some role in making it better?

Accountability is the backbone of action. Those with higher AQs hold themselves accountable for dealing with situations regardless of their cause. Those with lower AQs deflect accountability and most often feel victimized and helpless.

R = Reach

How far does the fallout of this situation reach into other areas of your work or life?

To what extent does the adversity extend beyond the situation at hand?

Keeping the fallout under control and limiting the reach of adversity is essential for efficient and effective problem solving. Those with higher AQs keep setbacks and challenges in their place, not letting them infest the healthy areas of their work and lives. Those with lower AQs tend to catastrophize, allowing a setback in one area to bleed into other, unrelated areas and become destructive.

E = Endurance

How long will the adversity endure?

Seeing beyond even enormous difficulties is an essential skill for maintaining hope. Those with higher AQs have the uncanny ability to see past the most interminable difficulties and maintain hope and optimism. Those with lower AQs see adversity as dragging on indefinitely, if not permanently.

©2006 Winston J. Brill & Associates. All rights reserved.

APPENDIX C: ADVERSITY QUOTES

- "Men do not stumble over mountains, but over molehills." — **Confucius**

- "Adversity is not a bad thing...It's a God thing!" — **Dina Rolle**

- "In the face of adversity you have three choices... You can let it DEFINE you, let it DESTROY you or let it STRENGTHEN YOU!" — **Tanya Masse**

- "Sometimes what makes us insecure and vulnerable becomes the fuel we need to be overachievers. The antidote for a snake bite is made from the poison, and the thing that made you go backward is the same force that will push you forward." — **T. D. Jakes**

- "One nation is weakened by a victory, another finds new forces in defeat." — **Antoine de Saint-Exupéry**

- "If you wish to break with tradition, learn your craft well, and embrace adversity." — **Soke Behzad Ahmadi**

- "Adversity does more than build character. It changes the way we see the world." — **Michael R. French**

- "Be strong and courageous. Fear not! God will grant you the strength to overcome any adversity." — **Lailah Gifty Akita**

- "The greater the adversity the greater the rewards." — **Matshona Dhliwayo**

- "The most beautiful people we have known are those who have known defeat, known suffering, known struggle, known loss, and have found their way out of the depths. These persons have an appreciation, sensitivity, and an understanding of life that fills them with compassion, gentleness, and a deep loving concern. Beautiful people do not just happen."
– **Elisabeth Kubler-Ross**

- "Nearly all men can stand adversity, but if you want to test a man's character, give him power."
– **Abraham Lincoln**

- "Never to suffer would never to have been blessed."
– **Edgar Allan Poe**

- "If the road is easy, you're likely going the wrong way."
– **Gordon B. Hinckley**

APPENDIX D: ACHIEVEMENT QUOTES

- "Keep on beginning and failing. Each time you fail, start all over again, and you will grow stronger until you have accomplished a purpose ... not the one you began with perhaps, but one you will be glad to remember." – **Anne Sullivan Macy**

- "My grandfather once told me that there were two kinds of people: those who do the work and those who take the credit. He told me to try to be in the first group; there was much less competition. "
  – **Indira Gandhi**

- "When obstacles arise, you change your direction to reach your goal; do not change your decision to get there." – **Zig Ziglar**

- "Permanence, perseverance and persistence in spite of all obstacles, discouragements, and impossibilities: it is this that in all things distinguishes the strong soul from the weak." –**Thomas Carlyle**

- "Start by doing what is necessary, then what is possible; and suddenly you are doing the impossible."
  – **Saint Francis of Assisi**

- "Experience is a hard teacher because she gives the test first, the lesson afterwards." – **Vernon Sanders Law**

- "Jumping at several small opportunities may get us there more quickly than waiting for one big one to come along." –**Hugh Allen**

- "Unless commitment is made, there are only promises and hopes... but no plans."– **Peter F. Drucker**

- "In all human affairs there are efforts, and there are results, and the strength of the effort is the measure of the result."
  – **James Allen**

- "Hard work does not guarantee success, but improves its chances." – **B. J. Gupta**

- "Achievement of your happiness is the only moral purpose of your life, and that happiness, not pain or mindless self-indulgence, is the proof of your moral integrity, since it is the proof and the result of your loyalty to the achievement of your values."
  – **Ayn Rand**

- "In the confrontation between the stream and the rock, the stream always wins- not through strength but by perseverance." – **H. Jackson Brown, Jr**.

- "The world is moving so fast these days that the man who says it can't be done is generally interrupted by someone doing it." – **Elbert Hubbard**

- "Destiny is not a matter of chance, it is a matter of choice; it is not a thing to be waited for, but a thing to be achieved." –**William Jennings Bryan**

- "The difference between a dream and achievement is an agenda." – **Hollis L. Green**

- "There is only one thing that makes a dream impossible to achieve: the fear of failure."– **Paulo Coelho**

- "Only those who attempt the absurd can achieve the impossible." –**Albert Einstein**

- "Nothing in the world is worth having or worth doing unless it means effort, pain, difficulty...I have never in my life envied a human being who led an easy life. I have envied a great many people who led difficult lives and led them well." **–Theodore Roosevelt**

- "It is amazing what you can accomplish if you do not care who gets the credit." **–Harry S. Truman**

- "Don't mistake activity with achievement." **–John Wooden**

- "To accomplish great things we must not only act, but also dream; not only plan, but also believe." **–Anatole France**

OTHER BOOKS BY THE AUTHOR

The Anapausis Partnership

– A Model of Philanthropy, Mentoring, and Coaching

ISBN: 978-1-935434-49-8

The book deals with common sense lessons and faith-based principles that result in a model of Philanthropy, Mentoring, and Coaching. It is a "How To" treatise in building both a relationship and advancing an agenda that benefits children, couples, faith-based groups, NGO'S, non-profit organizations, and family life. It is a true story of two individuals, who found each other amid their inspired mission to assist their homeland. It is a narrative of love and work, faith and worship, sacrament and service, stewardship and charity, teamwork and faithfulness. The pages are filled with common sense lessons that are later translated into faith-based principles and used to advance many projects for the benefit of the poor and needy.

God's Work Done God's Way

– You Don't Have to Make Headlines to Make a Difference

ISBN: 978-1-935434-60-3

Some see faith as a "vending machine," but the author shows not only the benefits of a faith-based life, but the obligations faith-based people to accomplish their work with guidance from Providence. He believes that to live a life with purpose and significance will be a good life that benefits others. This book presents a lifestyle that cares for the disadvantaged and meets the challenge to get others involved. Quality thoughts and moral values come from believing and behaving learned principles. It is not what one gather, but what is scatter that defines the quality of life.

Living a Life Larger Than Yourself

ISBN: 978-1-935434-62-7

The word "happiness" as it is used today it relies on the little word "hap" which means "good luck or by chance." Happenstance does not create a quality of life. Only purposeful behavior that is more than activities can bring the deep satisfaction of "happiness." Quality of life should not be confused with the standard of living, which is primarily income. The term "quality of life," as revealed in this book, is our positive intervention in the lives of the less fortunate.

Navigating the Challenges of Faith-based Behavior
– Conduct that Exhibits a Moral Course in Life

ISBN: 978-1-935434-64-1

A faith-based lifestyle determines both the course of action, the destination of the journey and provides a standard of behavior. Lifestyle provides intentionality of conduct and enables one to behave in a planned and deliberate way. The wise man Solomon was concerned about an empty life without permanent value that leads to frustration. He wrote, **"Pursue your course but know that God will judge your behavior."** (Ecclesiastes 11.9 EDOT) The value of a charted course relates to both the terminal objective and the time one has to travel toward stated goals. The design of this book illustrates in a nautical/sailing ship framework that there is a difference between **believe and behave.**

Ageing Has a Silver Lining
– Coping with Rainy Days

ISBN 978-1-935434-65-8

The purpose of the book is to improve the quality of life for seniors as they span the ageing process and move to their final decade of graceful ageing. The author deals with the difficulties of the ageing process, the senior living problems, the need for adequate eldercare facilities, and compassionate end of life care. The objective is to insure a Silver Lining to the clouds that surround the ageing process for seniors and their caregivers.

Adversity Leads to Achievement
– Learning to Surmount Difficulties

ISBN 978-1-935434-81-8

Adversity often becomes an open door of opportunity for achievement. An old adage about life stated *"It is not what happens in life, but what one does with what happens that makes a difference in the kind of person one becomes."* A saying attributed to Napoleon about the hazardous struggle of battle is appropriate, *"There is a time in every battle when both sides have lost --- victory belongs to the one who attacks first after this point of loss."* The lesson here was clear, when trouble comes one must take positive action to move past the difficulty. Loss can actually create the opportunity for gain. This common sense lesson from the past is most telling, *"Necessity is the mother of invention."* Difficulties can become stumbling stones to produce present failure or stepping stones to a positive future.

~

WWW.GEA-BOOKS.COM OR ANYWHERE GOOD BOOKS ARE SOLD

www.ingramcontent.com/pod-product-compliance
Lightning Source LLC
LaVergne TN
LVHW011423080426
835512LV00005B/233